Samuel French

Dangerous Music

The American Century Cycle Monologues

A Tool for Actors

by August Wilson

Edited by Constanza Romero & Zoe Wilson

SAMUELFRENCH.COM SAMUELFRENCH.CO.UK

ISBN 978-0-573-70642-4

United States and Canada
Info@SamuelFrench.com
1-866-598-8449
www.SamuelFrench.com

United Kingdom and Europe
Plays@SamuelFrench.co.uk
020-7255-4302
www.SamuelFrench.co.uk

TABLE OF CONTENTS

INTRODUCTION

Lights fade up. It's 2002. Two men stand outside the stage door entrance of a regional theater. They share a set of iPod headphones, a "V" of cord connects them. The younger man is white, baby-faced, late-twenties. The older man is twice that age, black, goateed, and wears a black felt Borsalino hat. The older man controls the iPod –

AUGUST. No, no, Todd, man, listen how she doesn't take a breath. She goes right from the verse into ... *(sings)* Somewhere over the rainbow.

TODD. Eva Cassidy, right?

AUGUST. Yeah, it's Eva Cassidy. You should know it's Eva Cassidy. I ain't talking about Eva Cassidy, I'm talking about that's how you learn about breath control. How you learn to listen to the way a singer finds their own way through a song. Here, I got another version ...

They listen awhile. Then August locks his brown eyes on Todd.

TODD. It's ... She's ... Well, Ella, she's –

AUGUST. So what you know it's Ella Fitzgerald. What I wanna know, what do you hear?

TODD. Her singing, she's clear.

AUGUST. Yeah, man, yeah! Ella's always gonna do it clean, hit every note clearly. Come on ...

TODD. Shouldn't we get back to rehearsal?

AUGUST. We're going to the record store. Music research. You need to hear Sarah Vaughn sing it. Sarah Vaughn makes every song bend her way.

Like "Over the Rainbow", each of these collected monologues are American Standards that can be sung a hundred and nine thousand different ways (at least!). So how do you plan to make them *bend your way*?

I suggest you work from the inside out. Read the plays. Listen. Everything you need to grow your interpretation is seeded in August's words. August taught me a hundred and nine thousand things (at least!). I'll share with you three:

> 1. Style is clarity.
> 2. You can never learn enough about your craft.
> 3. You can't get it wrong.

Academy Award-winner Viola Davis does not make August's words bend her way. I know it may seem that she does. But I've been privileged to be in the rehearsal room with her twice and can share that her virtuoso performances of August's work grow out of a monk-like devotion to his words and a relentless exploration of their intentions. *Style is clarity.*

While writing his masterpiece *Gem Of The Ocean*, August called one night after revisiting one of his favorite films, *The Battle of Algiers*. He was thrilled by learning new insights and techniques for making his own story about a political revolutionary more personal. *You can never learn enough about your craft.*

And if you put in the effort on #1 and #2, then you're prepared for #3. August was always terrified to speak in public. A sleepless night was behind every speech he gave. But he ultimately faced those fears, performing in his own one-man show, *How I Learned What I Learned*. Every night the backstage ritual was a hug followed by the mantra, *You can't get it wrong.*

Whether you're learning one of these monologues for an assignment, an audition, or to compete in the August Wilson Monologue Competition, before you step on stage, let me offer you the hug of an assurance that with proper preparation, *You can't get it wrong.* I promise that the exploration of August's work through performance will yield you fruit by enlarging your humanity.

Daily work with August didn't include coffee breaks. Rather, we would work toward the reward of our "iPod Time" (as shared in the opening of this introduction). August's iPod included a collection of artists you would expect, among them: Bessie Smith, Charley Patton, Bukka White, Sly and the Family Stone, and Smokey Robinson. But also on his iPod were artists as varied as Madeleine Peyroux, the Comedian Harmonists, Tom Waits, the Barenaked Ladies and even the punk Celtic band, the Dropkick Murphys. August had big arms for the world and deserves some big arms back.

As of this writing, my son, Evan August, is four-and-a-half years old. And while I don't wish for him to grow a minute too fast, I cannot wait to share with him his namesake's work that will be performed by some of you at August Wilson Monologue Competitions throughout the country. I want Evan to wrap big arms around these monologues and experience their universal power, their infinite variety rich with relationships of lovers, friends, fathers, sons, mothers, daughters, mentors, and students – the testimony of a culture that will thrive on the strength of what gets shared, what gets passed down through these words, these songs August Wilson left behind.

– *Todd Kreidler*
March 13, 2017

Todd Kreidler worked closely with August Wilson, developing his final three plays, co-conceiving and directing his one-man show. Todd co-founded with Kenny Leon, The August Wilson Monologue Competition.

THE LIFE OF AUGUST WILSON

1945

April 27: Born Frederick August Kittel in the Hill District of Pittsburgh, Pennsylvania

Mother: Daisy Wilson, an African American originally from North Carolina

Father: Frederick August Kittel, a German immigrant

1960

Drops out of high school in the ninth grade, when a teacher accuses him of plagiarizing a twenty-page paper on Napoleon

Continues his education by reading at the Carnegie Library

1962

Enlists in U.S. Army for three years; honorably discharged after one year

1963

Takes various jobs: short-order cook, gardener, dishwasher

1965

Discovers the blues when he buys a 78 rpm record, at The Salvation Army, of Bessie Smith's *Nobody Can Bake a Sweet Jelly Roll Like Mine*

Death of father, Frederick August Kittel

Buys first typewriter for $20

Changes name to August Wilson

1966

Joins the Centre Avenue Poets

1968

Co-founds Black Horizons Theatre

1969

Marries Brenda Burton in Pittsburgh

1970

Birth of daughter, Sakina Ansari

Early 1970s

Active in Black Arts movement, mainly reading and writing poetry

1976

Kuntu Repertory Theatre (formerly Black Horizons Theatre) stages *The Homecoming*

1978

Moves to St. Paul, Minnesota; gets a job writing short plays for the Science Museum of Minnesota

1980

Receives fellowship from The Playwrights Center in Minneapolis

1981

Marries Judy Oliver in Minnesota

1982

Allegheny Repertory Theater in Pittsburgh stages the premiere of *Jitney*

National Playwrights Conference at the Eugene O'Neill Theatre Center in Connecticut accepts *Ma Rainey's Black Bottom*, after previously rejecting *Jitney*

Meets Lloyd Richards, Artistic Director of both The National Playwrights Conference and Yale Repertory Theatre; he directs Wilson's first six plays on Broadway

1983

Death of mother, Daisy Wilson

Black Bart And The Sacred Hills, a musical satire, is professionally staged at Penumbra Theatre in St. Paul

1984

Ma Rainey's Black Bottom premieres at Yale Repertory Theatre, and moves to Broadway

Wins first New York Drama Critics Circle Best Play Award

1985

Ma Rainey's Black Bottom receives Wilson's first Tony Award nomination for Best Play

The original cast recording of *Ma Rainey's Black Bottom* wins Grammy Award for Best Spoken Word or Non-Musical Recording

Fences premieres at Yale Repertory Theatre

1986

Joe Turner's Come And Gone premieres at Yale Repertory Theatre

Fences receives American Theatre Critics Association Award

1987

Fences opens on Broadway, wins Tony Award for Best Play and New York Drama Critics Circle Award; sets record for first-year earnings of a non-musical on Broadway

Fences receives the Pulitzer Prize

The Piano Lesson premieres at Yale Repertory Theatre

1988

Joe Turner's Come And Gone opens on Broadway, wins New York Drama Critics Circle Award, and receives Tony nomination for Best Play

1989

The Piano Lesson receives American Theatre Critics Association Award

1990

The Piano Lesson opens on Broadway, wins New York Drama Critics Circle Award, and receives Tony Award nomination for Best Play

Receives second Pulitzer Prize for *The Piano Lesson*

Two Trains Running premieres at Yale Repertory Theatre

Relocates to Seattle

1991

Two Trains Running receives American Theatre Critics Association Award

1992

Two Trains Running opens on Broadway, wins New York Drama Critics Circle Award, and receives Tony Award nomination for Best Play

1994

Marries Constanza Romero in Seattle

1995

The Piano Lesson is broadcast for television's *Hallmark Hall of Fame*; Wilson receives an Emmy nomination for his adapted screenplay, and the show is recognized with the George Foster Peabody Award

Inducted into the American Academy of Arts and Letters

Seven Guitars premieres at Chicago's Goodman Theatre

1996

Seven Guitars arrives on Broadway; wins New York Drama Critics Circle Award, American Theatre Critics Association New Play Citation, and receives Tony nomination for Best Play

Controversial lecture, "The Ground On Which I Stand", electrifies the Theatre Communications Group's National Conference with a passionate call for separate Black theatre companies as essential to American theatre, emphasizing the need for equitable distribution of resources to support the work of Black theatre artists

Rewritten version of *Jitney* premieres at Pittsburgh Public Theater

1997

Takes part in major public debate in New York City with critic Robert Brustein on status of Black theatre in America

Birth of daughter, Azula Carmen Wilson

1998

Teaches playwriting at Dartmouth College; convenes Dartmouth Conference on African American Theater that leads to founding of the African Grove Institute of the Arts

1999

Awarded first and only High School diploma ever issued by the Carnegie Library of Pittsburgh

King Hedley II premieres at Pittsburgh Public Theater, marking the first play produced in the new O'Reilly Theater; a co-production with Seattle Repertory Theatre

2000

Jitney arrives in New York, the first August Wilson play staged Off-Broadway, wins New York Drama Critics Circle Award, and American Theatre Critics Association New Play Citation

2001

King Hedley II premieres on Broadway, receives American Theatre Critics Association New Play Citation and Tony nomination for Best Play

2002

Gem Of The Ocean premieres at Chicago's Goodman Theatre, inaugurating the new Albert Theatre

Jitney wins London's Olivier Award for the year's Best Play

2003

Ma Rainey's Black Bottom is revived on Broadway

Premieres one-man show, the autobiographical *How I Learned What I Learned*, at Seattle Repertory Theatre

2004

Gem Of The Ocean opens on Broadway; receives the American Theatre Critics Association New Play Citation

2005

Radio Golf premieres at Yale Repertory Theatre, fulfilling Wilson's goal of writing a play set in each decade of the twentieth century

Gem Of The Ocean receives Tony nomination for Best Play

June 14: Diagnosed with liver cancer

Revises *Radio Golf* for Mark Taper Forum in Los Angeles

October 2: Dies at age sixty in Seattle

October 8: Funeral held in Pittsburgh

The Virginia Theatre on Broadway is renamed the August Wilson Theatre

2006

Radio Golf receives American Theatre Critics Association New Play Citation

2007

Radio Golf premieres on Broadway and receives a Tony nomination for Best Play

Becomes most-awarded author in New York Drama Critics Circle history when *Radio Golf* receives Wilson's eighth award for Best American Play

Theatre Communications Group publishes *The August Wilson Century Cycle*, a ten-volume boxed edition, marking the never-before-achieved artistic ambition of creating a full cycle of plays

At the time of his death, August Wilson had been awarded a total of twenty-eight honorary degrees and many accolades and honors, among them the National Humanities Medal presented by President Bill Clinton, *TIME Magazine*'s America's Best Series: Best Playwright, New Dramatists Lifetime Achievement Award, and the Heinz Award. Posthumously, he received the Dramatists Guild Award for Lifetime Achievement and was inducted into the Theater Hall of Fame.

GEM OF THE OCEAN

Act 1, Scene 2

*Citizen Barlow has come to Pittsburgh from
Alabama hoping for a better life. He seeks
Aunt Ester's help to have his soul washed.
Aunt Ester, a spiritual healer, asks Citizen
where he is from. He shares his challenging
journey.*

CITIZEN. Alabama. I only been up here four weeks. When
I left Alabama they had all the roads closed to the colored people. I had to sneak out. Say they didn't want
anybody to leave. Say we had to stay there and work. I
told my mama I was going and she say okay. Told me,
"There a big world out there." I kissed her. She told me
she loved me and I left. I almost got caught a couple of
times. I had to go out the back way and find my own
roads. Took me almost two weeks. There was some
other people out on the road and we helped each other.
Me and a fellow named Roper Lee went over to the
mill. They say they was paying two dollars a day but
when we got there they say a dollar fifty. Then they say
we got to pay two dollars room and board. They sent us
over to a place the man say we got to put two dollars on
top of that. Then he put two men to a room with one
bed. The fellow I was with want to fight about it. I'm
just starting out I don't want no trouble. I told him I
would sleep on the floor. I wasn't planning on sleeping
there long. I'm just starting out sleeping there. I asked
one fellow what board meant. He say they supposed to
give you something to eat. They ain't give us nothing. I
say okay. I can't make them give me nothing. What I'm
gonna do? I got to eat. I bought a loaf of bread for a
dime. A bowl of soup cost ten cents around the corner.
I wasn't desperate. I had sixty-five cents to make it to
payday. I ate half the bread and say I would get a bowl
of soup tomorrow. Come payday they give me three

dollars say the rest go on my bill. I had to give the man what own the house two dollars. What I'm gonna do, Miss Tyler? I told the people at the mill I was gonna get another job. They said I couldn't do that 'cause I still owed them money and they was gonna get the police on me. I was gonna go to another city but then before I had a chance I killed a man. I don't know, Miss Tyler. I feel like I got a hole inside me. People say you can help me. I don't want to go to hell, Miss Tyler. My mama cry every time something bad happen to me.

Act 1, Scene 3

Caesar Wilks, the local constable, just arrested hundreds of black men rioting down at the mill. When Caesar meets Citizen, he lectures him on how to be a successful black man in the city.

CAESAR. Here ... here go a quarter. I'm gonna see what you do with that. These niggers take and throw their money away in the saloon and get mad when it's gone. I give one fellow a quarter and he turn around and give it to the candy man. I say he could have did something with that quarter. It wasn't much but it was twenty-five cents more than he had. He took and threw it away. He can't see past his nose. He can't see it's all set up for him to do anything he want. See, he could have took and bought him a can of shoe polish and got him a rag. If he could see that far he'd look up and find twenty-five dollars in his pocket. Twenty-five dollars buys you an opportunity. You don't need but five dollars to get in the crap game. That's five opportunities he done threw away. The candy man gonna get him a bigger wagon and another five pound of sugar. He gonna be digging a ditch the rest of his life. I'm gonna see what you do. You turn that twenty-five cents into five dollars and you come and see me and I'll give you a job.

I can see you one of them hardheaded niggers. You have to bust you upside the head a couple of times. Then you straighten up. You watch yourself. See, 'cause you just got on my list. I told you I'm the boss man around here. Ask anybody. They'll tell you who Caesar is.

Act 1, Scene 3

As the constable, Caesar is feared and judged by his community for being harsh on criminals. Caesar believes that he has to keep order. He insists that he is not to blame for the drowning of a man who was escaping from the law.

CAESAR. I'd say I didn't do it too if the law was after me. You arrest somebody for loitering and they'll swear they ain't standing there. That don't mean nothing to me 'cause he say he didn't do it. I had witnesses. Five hundred people standing around watching the man drown. I tried to break it up. Get them to go home. But they wanna stand around and watch a damn fool drown himself in the river. I tried to save him but he ain't had enough sense to save himself. People wanna blame me but I got to keep order. Just like them niggers wanna riot over a bucket of nails. Talking about they ain't going to work. Talking about closing the mill down. They don't understand the mill is what hold everything together. If you close down the mill the city would be in chaos. The city needs that tin. They need that tin in Philadelphia. They need it in Detroit and Cincinnati. Industry is what drive the country. Without industry wouldn't nobody be working. That tin put people to work doing other things. These niggers can't see that. They ought to be glad the mill is there. If it wasn't for the mill these niggers wouldn't have no way to pay their rent. Close down the mill and wait and see what happen then. I'll tell you. A hundred niggers is going to jail for trying to steal something. That's what's gonna happen. A hundred niggers is going to jail for loitering. A hundred niggers is going to jail for disturbing the peace after they get mad and start fighting each other. Five hundred babies is gonna go hungry. You gonna have a hundred new prostitutes. People gonna be living on the streets begging for a dime. And all because some damn fool took it upon himself to steal a bucket of nails and run and jump in the goddamn river. You close down the mill you ain't got nothing. Them niggers can't see that. Want to blame me. You know whose fault it is. I'll tell you whose fault it is. It's Abraham Lincoln's fault. He ain't had no idea what he was doing. He didn't know like I know. Some of these niggers was better off in slavery. They don't know how to act otherwise. You try and do something nice for niggers and it'll backfire on you every time. You try and give them an opportunity by giving them a job and they take and throw it away. Talking about they ain't going to work.

Act 1, Scene 4

Citizen has asked Black Mary to come to his room. Here Black Mary sarcastically offers herself to him, then tells him he is no different than the other men who have come and gone in her life.

BLACK MARY. Here, Mr. Citizen. Here.

(Citizen embraces her. Black Mary lays her head on his chest.)

You got a woman in your hands. Now what? What you got? What you gonna do? Time ain't long, Mr. Citizen. A woman ain't but so many times filled up. What you gonna do? What you gonna fill me up with? Love? Happiness? Peace? What you got, Mr. Citizen? I seen it all. You got something new? Fill me up, Mr. Citizen. What you got for me, you got something I ain't seen? Come on. What can I be without you?

(Citizen steps out of her embrace. Black Mary returns to chopping vegetables.)

Leroy. And John. And Cujoe. And Sam. And Robert. One after the other they come and they go. You can't hold on to none of them. They slip right through your hands. They use you up and you can't hold them. They all the time taking till it's gone. They ain't tried to put nothing to it. They ain't got nothing in their hand. They ain't got nothing to add to it. They too busy taking. They taking 'cause they need. You can't blame them for that. They so full of their needs they can't see you. Now here you come. You don't even know what you need. All you see is a woman. You can't see nothing else. You can't think nothing else. That blinds you.

(Black Mary turns to him. A new thought occurs to her.)

Okay Mr. Citizen. I'll come to your room tonight. But the morning got to come, Mr. Citizen. What you got then? You tell me tomorrow. You wake up and look at your hands and see what you got.

Act 1, Scene 5

Black Mary is washing Aunt Ester's feet and Aunt Ester is smoking a pipe. In this moment, Aunt Ester sees that Black Mary is still trying to figure out life. She shares her origin story, hoping to inspire Black Mary to carry her legacy.

AUNT ESTER. You think you supposed to know everything. Life is a mystery. Don't you know life is a mystery? I see you still trying to figure it out. It ain't all for you to know. It's all an adventure. That's all life is. But you got to trust that adventure. I'm on an adventure. I been on one since I was nine years old. That's how old I was when my mama sent me to live with Miss Tyler. Miss Tyler gave me her name. Ester Tyler. I don't tell nobody what I was called before that. The only one know that is my mama. I stayed right on there with her till she dies. Miss Tyler passed it on to me. If you ever make up your mind I'm gonna pass it on to you. People say it's too much to carry. But I told myself somebody got to carry it. Miss Ester carried it. Carried it right up till the day she died. I didn't run from it. I picked it up and walked with it. I got a strong memory. I got a long memory. People say you crazy to remember. But I ain't afraid to remember. I try to remember out loud. I keep my memories alive. I feed them. I got to feed them otherwise they'd eat me up. I got memories go way back. I'm carrying them for a lot of folk. All the old-timey folks. I'm carrying their memories and I'm carrying my own. If you don't want it I got to find somebody else. I'm getting old. Going on three hundred years now. That's what Miss Tyler told me. Two hundred eighty-five by my count.

Act 1, Scene 5

*As Aunt Ester prepares to wash Citizen's soul,
she tells a tale about a man who raised pigs
to help Citizen find renewed meaning in his
life.*

AUNT ESTER. I know a man used to raise pigs. Great big old
pigs. To him the pig was the beginning of everything.
And it was the end of everything. Wherever he looked
he saw pigs. He saw pigs in the sky and he saw pigs on
the ground. To him the pig was the center of his life.
One day another man come along and killed all his pigs.
He lost everything he had. He lost the center of his life
'cause it wasn't inside him. It wasn't something nobody
could take away. See, Mr. Citizen, right now that bucket
of nails is at the center of your life. You only have one
life, Mr. Citizen. It's your life. Can't nobody else claim
it. You ain't never gonna forget that man who jumped
in the river. There are times when it will come and take
hold of you and shake you. There ain't nothing you can
do about that. It's them in-between times that you can
do something about. You got to find something else to
be at the center of your life. You got to find out why it
was important for Garrett Brown to die rather than to
take his thirty days.

Act 2, Scene 1

Aunt Ester is getting ready to take Citizen on a symbolic journey through the middle passage. She hopes that by reconnecting him to his past, she can inspire him to face the future.

AUNT ESTER. Some people don't like adventure, Mr. Citizen. They stay home. Like me. I done seen all the adventure I want to see. I been across the water. I seen both sides of it. I know about the water. The water has its secrets the way the land has its secrets. Some know about the land. Some know about the water. But there is some that know about the land and the water. They got both sides of it. Then you got the fire. That's a special one. It's got lots of secrets. Fire will heal and kill. It's tricky like that. I can talk about the land and I can talk about the fire. But I don't talk about the water. There was a time, Mr. Citizen, when God moved on the water. And sometime he moves on the land. Is he moving now? We don't know. We can't all the time see it.

Take a look at this map, Mr. Citizen. See that right there … that's a city. It's only a half mile by a half mile but that's a city. It's made of bones. Pearly white bones. All the buildings and everything is made of bones. I seen it. I been there, Mr. Citizen. My mother live there. I got an aunt and three uncles live down there in that city made of bones. You want to go there, Mr. Citizen? I can take you there if you want to go. That's the center of the world. In time it will all come to light. The people made a kingdom out of nothing. They were the people that didn't make it across the water. They sat down right there. They say, "Let's make a kingdom. Let's make a city of bones." The people got a burning tongue, Mr. Citizen. Their mouths are on fire with song. That water can't put it out. That song is powerful. It rise up and come across the water. Ten thousand tongues and ten thousand chariots coming across the water. They on their way Mr. Citizen. They coming across the water. Ten thousand hands and feet coming across the water. They on their way. I came across that ocean, Mr. Citizen. I cried. I had lost everything. Everything I had ever known in this life I lost that. I cried a ocean of tears. Did you ever lose anything like that, Mr. Citizen? Where you so lost the only thing that can guide you is the stars. That's all I had left. Everything I had ever known was gone to me. The only thing I had was the stars. I say well I got something. I wanted to hold on to them so I started naming them. I named them after my children. I say there go Scefus and that's Jasper and that's Cecilia, and that big one over there that's Junebug. You ever look at the stars, Mr. Citizen? I bet you seen my Junebug and didn't even know it. You come by here sometime when the stars are out and I'll show you my Junebug. You come by anytime you want. You got the stars but it's that wind what drive the boat, Mr. Citizen. Without the wind it would just sit there. But who drives the wind? What god drives the wind? That's what I asked myself but I didn't have no answer. So I just started singing. Just singing quietly to myself some song my mother had taught me. After that it was all right for a little while. But the wind did drive the boat right across the water. What it was driving me to I didn't know. That's what made it so hard. And I didn't have my mother to tell me. That made it harder.

You see that, Mr. Citizen. That's a boat. You gonna take a ride on that boat.

Act 2, Scene 2

After Citizen claims that debt is worse than slavery, Solly, a former slave, tells Citizen about his own journey to freedom and his commitment to helping ride the Underground Railroad.

SOLLY. Ain't nothing worse than slavery! I know. I was there. Dark was the night and cold was the ground. Look at that ...

(He hands Citizen a chain link.)

That's my good luck piece. That piece of chain used to be around my ankle. They tried to chain me down but I beat them on that one. I say I'm gonna keep this to remember by. I been lucky ever since. I beat them on a lot of things. I beat them when I got away. I had some people who helped me. They helped show me the way and looked out for me. I got all the way to Canada. There was eight of us. I was in Canada in 1857. I stood right there in Freedomland. That's what they called it. Freedomland. I asked myself "What I'm gonna do?" I looked around. I didn't see nothing for me. I tried to feel different but I couldn't. I started crying. I hadn't cried since my daddy knocked me down for crying when I was ten years old. I breathed in real deep to taste the air. It didn't taste no different. The man what brought us over the border tried to talk with me. I just sat right down on the ground and started crying. I told him say "I don't feel right." It didn't feel right being in freedom and my mama and all the other people still in bondage. Told him, "I'm going back with you." I stopped crying soon as I said that. I joined the Underground Railroad. Look at that ...

(Shows Citizen his stick)

That's sixty-two notches. That's sixty-two people I

carried to freedom. I was looking to make it sixty-three when Abraham Lincoln come along and changed all that. Him and General Grant. I never did join the Union Army but I showed them where to go. I know all the routes. Me and Eli worked together many a time.

Act 2, Scene 3

Black Mary is wearing a blue dress which sparks Citizen's memory. He met a woman once who wore a blue dress at a dance. She couldn't stop crying.

CITIZEN. You got on that blue dress. I met this gal at a dance one time had on a blue dress. She had on a blue dress and she had her hair slicked back. Her mouth made her face look pretty. She was dancing and she had tears in her eyes. I asked her why she was crying. She said she was lonesome. I told her I couldn't fix that but if she wanted somebody to walk her home after the dance I'd walk her. See that she got home safe. She thanked me and went on crying. Say she felt better, and after the dance I could walk her home since I was going that way. She had a good time dancing with some of the other men. I danced with her some more. She was smiling but she still had tears in her eyes. After the dance I walked her home. I seen at the dance that she had a nice way about her. When she was walking home she put her hand in mine. She asked me did I want to stay the night. I told her yes. I told her I was at the dance looking for a woman. She asked me why didn't I tell her, we could have saved each other some time. I woke up in the morning and she was laying there crying. I didn't ask her about it. I didn't try and stop her. I lay there a while trying to figure out what to do. I ended up holding her in my arms. She started crying some more. I held her a while and then I left. I said good-bye to her and started walking away. She was standing in the door. I looked back and she was standing so she fit right in the middle of the door. I couldn't see if she was crying. She kind of waved at me. I got a little further on and turned and looked back and she was still there. Look like she had got smaller like she might have sat down in the doorway. That's what it looked like to me. I can still see her standing there. Had a green door and I can see her standing in it. I don't know what happened to her. I'd like to look on her face again. Just to know that she all right and if she stopped crying. If I could see her face I believe that would be enough.

Act 2, Scene 3

*Black Mary has been living and working for
Aunt Ester for three years. Aunt Ester is con-
stantly nagging her about how she cooks and
cleans. In this moment, Black Mary stands
up for herself and tells Aunt Ester how things
will be from here on out. With this stand,
she makes an important decision about her
future.*

BLACK MARY. Here! You cook it! You turn it down! I can't
do everything the way you want me to. I'm not you. You
act like there ain't no other way to do nothing. I got my
own way of doing things. I like the fire high. That's the
way I cook. You like it down. That's the way you cook. If
you ain't cooking you ain't got nothing to say about it.
All you got to worry about is the eating.

It's been three years now I can't do nothing to satisfy
you. I may as well lay down somewhere and forget
about it. You got something to say about everything.
Turn the fire down. Wash the greens in the other pot.
Shake that flour off that chicken. Tuck in the corners
of the sheets. That too much starch. That ain't enough
salt. I'm tired of it! Your way ain't always the best way. I
got my own way and that's the way I'm doing it. If I stay
around here I'm doing it my own way.

Act 2, Scene 4

*Black Mary's brother, Caesar, has shot and
killed Solly Two Kings. Black Mary recalls
the time when her brother was a good man.
She renounces him as her brother.*

BLACK MARY. Caesar, I gave you everything. Even when
I didn't have to give you. I made every way for you.
I turned my eyes away. I figured if I didn't see it I
couldn't hold fault. If I held fault I couldn't hold on to
my love for you. But now you standing in the light and
I can't turn away no more. I remember you when you
was on the other side of the law. That's my brother. The
one selling hoecakes off the back of a wagon. The one
that helped Mrs. Robinson and the kids when nobody
else would. That's my brother. The one who used to get
out of bed to take me to school. The one who believed
everybody had the same right to life ... the same right to
whatever there was in life they could find useful. That's
my brother. I don't know who you are. But you not my
brother. You hear me, Caesar? You not my brother.

JOE TURNER'S
COME AND GONE

Act 1, Scene 1

Bynum, a root-worker, wants Rutherford Selig, a people finder, to find a "shining man", a man who has made true peace with his past.

BYNUM. This fellow don't have no name. I call him John 'cause it was up around Johnstown where I seen him. I ain't even so sure he's one special fellow. That shine could pass on to anybody. He could be anybody shining.

He's just a man I seen out on the road. He ain't had no special look. Just a man walking toward me on the road. He come up and asked me which way the road went. I told him everything I knew about the road, where it went and all, and he asked me did I have anything to eat 'cause he was hungry. Say he ain't had nothing to eat in three days. Well, I never be out there on the road without a piece of dried meat. Or an orange or an apple. So I give this fellow an orange. He take and eat that orange and told me to come and go along the road a little ways with him, that he had something he wanted to show me. He had a look about him made me wanna go with him, see what he gonna show me.

We walked on a bit and it's getting kind of far from where I met him when it come up on me all of a sudden, we wasn't going the way he had come from, we was going back my way. Since he said he ain't knew nothing about the road, I asked him about this. He say he had a voice inside him telling him which way to go and if I come and go along with him he was gonna show me the Secret of Life. Quite naturally I followed him. A fellow that's gonna show you the Secret of Life ain't to be taken lightly. We get near this bend in the road … We get near this bend in the road and he told me to hold out my hands. Then he rubbed them together with his and I look down and see they had blood on them ...

I look down and see they had blood on them. Told me to take and rub it all over me, say that was a way of cleaning myself. Then we went around the bend in that road. Got around that bend and it seem like all of a sudden we ain't in the same place. Turn around that bend and everything look like it was twice as big as it was. The trees and everything bigger than life. Sparrows big as eagles. I turned around to look at this fellow and he had this light coming out of him. I had to cover up my eyes to keep from being blinded. He shining like new money with that light. He shined until all the light seemed like it seeped out of him and then he was gone and I was by myself in this strange place where everything was bigger than life.

I wandered around there looking for that road, trying to find my way back from this big place, and I looked over and seen my daddy standing there. He was the same size he always was, except for his hands and his mouth. He had a great big old mouth that looked like it took up his whole face and his hands were as big as hams. Look like they was too big to carry around. My daddy called me to him. Said he had been thinking about me and it grieved him to see me in the world carrying other people's songs and not having one of my own. Told me he was gonna show me how to find my song. Then he carried me further into this big place until we come to this ocean. Then he showed me something I ain't got words to tell you. If you stand to witness it, you done seen something there. I stayed in that place awhile and my daddy taught me the meaning of this thing that I had seen and showed me how to find my song. I asked him about the shiny man and he tole me he was the One Who Goes Before and Shows the Way. Say there was lots of shiny men and if I ever saw one again before I died that I would know that my song had been accepted and worked its full power in the world and I could lay down and die a happy man. A man who done left his mark on life. On the way people cling to each other out of the truth they find in themselves. Then he showed me how to get back to the road. I came out to where everything was its own size and I had my song. I had the Binding Song. I choose that song because that's what I seen most when I was traveling, people walking away and leaving one another. So I takes the power of my song and binds them together.

Been binding people ever since. That's why they call me Bynum. Just like glue I sticks people together

Act 1, Scene 1

Jeremy believes that he has the world in his hand. He tells Bynum that he doesn't play in guitar contests because, once, he participated in a contest where a white judge couldn't tell the difference between good and bad guitar playing.

JEREMY. Naw, he ain't beat me. I was sitting at home just fixing to sit down and eat when somebody come up to my house and got me. Told me there's a white fellow say he was gonna give a prize to the best guitar player he could find. I take up my guitar and go down there and somebody had gone up and got Bobo Smith and brought him down there. Him and another fellow called Hooter. Old Hooter couldn't play no guitar, he do more hollering than playing, but Bobo could go at it awhile.

This fellow standing there say he the one that was gonna give the prize and me and Bobo started playing for him. Bobo play something and then I'd try to play something better than what he played. Old Hooter, he just holler and bang at the guitar. Man was the worse guitar player I ever seen. So me and Bobo played and after awhile I seen where he was getting the attention of this white fellow. He'd play something and while he was playing it he be slapping on the side of the guitar, and that made it sound like he was playing more than he was. So I started doing it too. White fellow ain't knew no difference. He ain't knew as much about guitar playing as Hooter did. After we play while, the white fellow called us to him and said he couldn't make up his mind, say all three of us was the best guitar player and we'd have to split the prize between us. Then he give us twenty-five cents. That's eight cents apiece and a penny on the side. That cured me of playing contest to this day.

Act 1, Scene 1

*Mattie seeks Bynum's help to make her man,
Jack Carper, come back to her. Jack left
Mattie, saying she was cursed, after both of
their children died soon after their birth.*

MATTIE. Make him come back to me. Make his feet say my
name on the road. I don't care what happens. Make
him come back.

He go by Jack Carper. He was born in Alabama then
he come to West Texas and find me and we come here.
Been here three years before he left. Say I had a curse
prayer on me and he started walking down the road
ain't never come back. Somebody told me, say you can
fix things like that.

Ain't said nothing. Just started walking. I could see
where he disappeared. Didn't look back. Just keep
walking. Can you fix it so he come back? I ain't got no
curse prayer on me I know I ain't.

'Cause the babies died. Me and Jack had two babies.
Two little babies that ain't lived two months before they
died. He say it's because somebody cursed me not to
have babies.

Jack done gone off and you telling me to forget about
him. All my life I been looking for somebody to stop
and stay with me. I done already got too many things
to forget about. I take Jack Carper's hand and it feel
so rough and strong. Seem like he's the strongest man
in the world the way he hold me. Like he's bigger than
the whole world and can't nothing bad get to me. Even
when he act mean sometimes he still make everything
seem okay in the world. Like there's part of it that
belongs to you. Now you telling me to forget about
him?

Act 1, Scene 3

Jeremy has convinced Mattie to move into the boarding house with him. Bynum quickly lends some advice about how to truly appreciate a woman.

BYNUM. You just can't look at it like that. You got to look at the whole thing. Now you take a fellow go out there, grab hold to a woman and think he got something 'cause she sweet and soft to the touch. Alright. Touching's a part of life. It's in the world like everything else. Touching's nice. It feels good. But you can lay you hand upside a horse or a cat, and that feels good too. What's the difference? When you grab hold to a woman, you got you something there. You got a whole world there. You got a way of life kicking up under your hand. That woman can take and make you feel like something. I ain't just talking about in the way of jumping off into bed together and rolling around with each other. Anybody can do that. When you grab hold to that woman and look at the whole thing and see what you got ... why she can take and make something out of you. Your mother was a woman. That's enough right there to show you what a woman is. Enough to show you what she can do. She made something out of you. Taught you converse, and all about how to take care of yourself, how to see where you at and where you going tomorrow, how to look out to see what's coming in the way of eating, and what to do with yourself when you get lonesome. That's a mighty thing she did. But you just can't look at a woman to jump off into bed with her. That's a foolish thing to ignore a woman like that.

Alright. Let's try it this way. Now you take a ship. Be out there on the water traveling about. You out there on the ship sailing to and from. And then you see some land. Just like you see a woman walking down the street. You see that land and it don't look like nothing but a line out there on the horizon. That's all it is when you first see it. A line that cross your path out there on the horizon. Now, a smart man know when he see that land, it ain't just a line setting out there. He know that if you get off the water to go take a good look ... Why there's a whole world right there. A whole world with everything imaginable under the sun. Anything you can think of you can find on that land. Same with a woman. A woman is everything a man need. That's all he need to live on. You give me some water and berries and if there ain't nothing else I can live a hundred years.

(Jeremy tries to interrupt. Bynum cuts him off.)

See, you just like a man looking at the horizon from a ship. You just seeing a part of it. But it's a blessing when you learn to look at a woman and see in maybe just a few strands of her hair, the way her cheek curves ... to see in that everything there is out of life to be gotten. It's a blessing to see that. You know you done right and proud by your mother to see that. But you got to learn it. My telling you ain't gonna mean nothing. You got to learn how to come to your own time and place with a woman.

Act 2, Scene 1

*Molly Cunningham just arrived at the board-
ing house and sees Mattie doing Jeremy's
laundry. She shares her philosophy with
Mattie: don't trust men and don't have their
babies.*

MOLLY. I don't trust none of these men. Jack or nobody
else. These men liable to do anything. They wait just
until they get one woman tied and locked up with them
... then they look around to see if they can get another
one. Molly don't pay them no mind. One's just as good
as the other if you ask me. I ain't never met no man
that meant nobody no good.

These men make all these babies, then run off and
leave you to take care of them. Talking about they want
to see what's on the other side of the hill. I make sure
I don't get no babies. My mama taught me how to do
that.

Molly Cunningham ain't gonna be tied down with no
babies. Had me one man who I thought had some
love in him. Come home one day and he packing his
trunk. Told me the time comes when even the best of
friends must part. Say he was gonna send me a Special
Delivery some old day. I watched him out the window
when he carried that old trunk out and down to the
train station. Said if he was gonna send me a Special
Delivery I wasn't gonna be there to get it. I done found
out the harder you try to hold onto them, the easier it
is for some gal to pull them away. Molly done learned
that. That's why I don't trust nobody but the good Lord
above, and I don't love nobody but my mama.

Act 2, Scene 2

While playing dominoes, Bynum begins to sing a song about Joe Turner. This upsets Loomis, and he asks Bynum to stop. But Bynum knows this is because Loomis has forgotten his song.

BYNUM. I can tell from looking at you. My daddy taught me how to do that. Say when you look at a fellow, if you taught yourself to look for it, you can see his song written on him. Tell you what kind of man he is in the world. Now I can look at you, Mr. Loomis, and see you a man who done forgot his song. Forgot how to sing it. A fellow forget that and he forget who he is. Forget how he's supposed to mark down life. Now I used to travel all up and down this road and that ... looking here and there. Searching. Just like you, Mr. Loomis ... I didn't know what I was searching for. The only thing I knew was something was keeping me dissatisfied. Something wasn't making my heart smooth and easy. Then one day my daddy gave me a song. That song had a weight to it that was hard to handle. That song was hard to carry. I fought against it. Didn't want to accept that song. I tried to find my daddy to give him back the song. But I found out it wasn't his song. It was my song. It had come from way deep inside me. I looked way back in my memory and gathered up pieces and snatches of things to make that song. I was making it up out of myself. And that song helped me on the road. Made it smooth to where my footsteps didn't bite back at me. All the time that song getting bigger and bigger. That song growing with each step of the road. It got so I used all of myself up in the making of that song. Then I was the song in search of itself. That song rattling in my throat and I'm looking for it. See, Mr. Loomis, when a man forgets his song he goes off in search of it ... till he finds out he's got it with him all the time. That's why I can tell you one of Joe Turner's niggers. 'Cause you forgot how to sing your song.

Act 2, Scene 2

Bynum tells Loomis that he knows his history. Loomis recounts his torturous seven-year enslavement after he was captured by Joe Turner's men.

LOOMIS. Had a whole mess of men he catched. Just go out hunting regular like you go out hunting possum. He catch you and go home to his wife and family. Ain't thought about you going home to yours. Joe Turner catched me when my little girl was just born. Wasn't nothing but a little baby sucking on her mama's titty when he catched me. Joe Turner catched me in nineteen hundred and one. Kept me seven years until nineteen hundred and eight, kept everybody seven years. He'd go out hunting and bring back forty men at a time. And keep them seven years.

I was walking down this road in this little town outside of Memphis. Come up on these fellows gambling. I was a deacon in the Abundant Life Church. I stopped to preach to these fellows to see if I could turn some of them from their sinning when Joe Turner – brother of the Governor of the Great Sovereign State of Tennessee – swooped down and grabbed everybody there. Kept us all seven years.

My wife Martha gone from me after Joe Turner catched me. Got out from under Joe Turner on his birthday. Me and forty other men put in our seven years and he let us go on his birthday. I made it back to Henry Thompson's place where me and Martha was sharecropping and Martha's gone. She taken my little girl and left her with her mama and took off North. We been looking for her ever since. That's been going on four years now we been looking. That's the only thing I know how to do. I just wanna see her face so I can get me a starting place in the world. The World got to start somewher⟋ what I been looking for. I been wandering a long⟋ in somebody else's world. When I find my wife tha⟋ the making of my own.

Act 2, Scene 3

'ts Mattie after Jeremy leaves
'use with another woman. She
to stay away from Bynum's
' powers and tries to instill in
... a positive way to look at life.

BERTHA. If I was you, Mattie, I wouldn't go getting all tied up with Bynum in that stuff. That kind of stuff, even if it do work for awhile, it don't last. That just get people more mixed up than they is already. And I wouldn't waste my time fretting over Jeremy either. I seen it coming. I seen it when she first come here. She that kind of woman run off with the first man got a dollar to spend on her. Jeremy just young. He don't know what he getting into. That gal don't mean him no good. She's just using him to keep from being by herself. That's the worse kind of a man you can have. You ought to be glad to wash him out of your hair. I done seen all kind of men. I done seen them come and go through here. Jeremy ain't had enough to him for you. You need a man who's got some understanding and who willing to work with that understanding to come to the best he can. You got your time coming. You just tries too hard and can't understand why it don't work for you. Trying to figure it out don't do nothing but give you a troubled mind. Don't no man want a woman with a troubled mind.

You get all that trouble off your mind and just when it look like you ain't never gonna find what you want … you look up and it's standing right there. That's how I met my Seth. You gonna look up one day and find everything you want standing right in front of you. Been twenty-seven years now since that happened to me. But life ain't no happy-go-lucky time where everything be just like you want it. You got your time coming.

Act 2, Scene 5

*Martha speaks to her husband, Harold
Loomis, for the first time in more than seven
years. Martha explains why she could not
wait for him while he has enslaved by Joe
Turner.*

MARTHA. I didn't leave her motherless, Harold. Reverend
Tolliver wanted to move the church up North 'cause of
all the trouble the colored folks was having down there.
Nobody knew what was gonna happen traveling them
roads. We didn't even know if we was gonna make it
up here or not. I left her with my mama so she be safe.
That was better than dragging her out on the road
having to duck and hide from people. Wasn't no telling
what was gonna happen to us. I didn't leave her motherless in the world. I been looking for you. Harold, I
didn't know if you was ever coming back. They told me
Joe Turner had you and my whole world split half in
two. My whole life shattered. It was like I had poured it
in a cracked jar and it all leaked out the bottom. When
it go like that there ain't nothing you can do to put it
back together. You talking about Henry Thompson's
place like I'm still gonna be there working the land by
myself. How I'm gonna do that? You wasn't gone but
two months and Henry Thompson kicked me off his
land and I ain't had no place to go but to my mama's. I
stayed and waited there for five years before I woke up
one morning and decided that you was dead. Even if
you weren't, you were dead to me. I wasn't gonna carry
you with me no more. So I killed you in my heart. I
buried you. I mourned you. And then I picked up what
was left and went on to make life without you. I was a
young woman with life at my beckon. I couldn't drag
you behind me like a sack of cotton.

Act 2, Scene 5

Finding his wife after so many years, Loomis is finally able to have closure, and is free to start his life again. He leaves Zonia with her mother knowing that, at this stage of her life, this young girl needs her mother.

LOOMIS. I just been waiting to look on your face to say my goodbye. That goodbye got so big at times, seem like it was gonna swallow me up. Like Jonah in the whale's belly I sat up in that goodbye for four years. That goodbye kept me out on the road searching. Not looking on women in their houses. It kept me bound up to the road. All the time the goodbye swelling up in my chest till I'm about to bust. Now that I see your face I can say my goodbye and make my own world.

Martha ... here go your daughter. I tried to take care of her. See that she had something to eat. See that she was out of the elements. Whatever I know I tried to teach her. Now she need to learn from her mother whatever you got to teach her. That way she won't be no one-sided person.

Zonia, you go live with your mama. She a good woman. You go on with her and listen to her good. You my daughter and I love you like a daughter. I hope to see you again in the world somewhere. I'll never forget you.

MA RAINEY'S BLACK BOTTOM

Act 1, Scene 1

Slow Drag, the bass player in Ma Rainey's band, tells his bandmates the story of a man in Alabama who "sold his soul to the devil".

SLOW DRAG. Eliza Cotter is one of them. Alright. The man living up there in an old shack on Ben Foster's place, shoeing mules and horses, making them charms and things in secret. He hooked up with the devil. Showed one day all fancied out with just the finest clothes you ever seen on a colored man ... dressed just like one of them crackers ... and carrying this bag with them papers and things in. Alright. Had a pocketful of money, just living the life of a rich man. Ain't done no more work or nothing. Just had him a string of women he run around with and throw his money away on. Bought him a big fine house ... well, it wasn't that big, but it did have one of them white picket fences around it. Used to hire a man once a week just to paint that fence. Messed around there and one of the fellows of them gals he was messing with got fixed on him wrong and Eliza killed him. And he laughed about it. Sheriff come and arrest him, and then let him go. And he went around in that town laughing about killing this fellow. Trial come up, and the judge cut him loose. He must have been in converse with the devil, too ... 'cause he cut him loose and give him a bottle of whiskey! Folks ask what done happened to make him change, and he'd tell them straight out he done sold his soul to the devil and asked them if they wanted to sell theirs 'cause he could arrange it for them. Preacher see him coming, used to cross on the other side of the road. He'd just stand there and laugh at the preacher and call him a fool to his face.

Act 1, Scene 1

Toledo, the oldest member of the band, explains why the black man is now, in 1927, a "leftover of history". He wants black people to understand their past in order to determine their self-worth in the future.

TOLEDO. Now I'm gonna show you how this goes ... where you just a leftover from history. Everybody come from different places in Africa, right? Come from different tribes and things. Soon awhile they began to make one big stew. You had the carrots, the peas, and potatoes and what not over here. And over there, you had the meat, the nuts, the okra, corn ... and then you mix it up and let it cook right through to get the flavors flowing together ... then you got one thing. You got a stew. Now you take and eat the stew. You take and make your history with that stew. Alright. Now it's over. Your history's over and you done ate the stew. But you look around and you see some carrots over here, some potatoes over there. That stew's still there. You done made your history and it's still there. You can't eat it all. So what you got? You got some leftovers. That's what it is. You got some leftovers and you can't do nothing with it. You already making you another history ... cooking you another meal, and you don't need them leftovers no more. What to do?

See, we's the leftovers. The colored man is the leftovers. Now what's the colored man gonna do with himself? That's what we waiting to find out. But first we gotta know we the leftovers.

Now, who knows that? You find me a nigger that knows that and I'll turn any which-a-way you want me to. I'll bend over for you. You ain't gonna find that. And that's what the problem is. The problem ain't with the white

man. The white man know you just a leftover. 'Cause
he the one who done the eating and he know what he
done ate. But we don't know that we been took and
made history out of. Done went and filled the white
man's belly and now he's full and tired and wants you to
get out the way and let him be by himself. Now, I know
what I'm talking about. And if you wanna find out, you
just ask Mr. Irvin what he had yesterday for supper.
And if he's an honest white man ... which is asking for
a whole heap of a lot ... he'll tell you he done ate your
black ass and if you please, I'm full up with you ... so go
on and get off the plate and let me eat something else.

Act 1, Scene 1

Ambitious and temperamental, Levee is the trumpet player in Ma's band. The band taunts Levee after he says "yessir" to the white record producer. In response, Levee tells them a harrowing story from his childhood that shaped the real way he feels about the "white man".

Optional cut for time purposes: Begin with "My mama was frying up some chicken when them mens come in that house."

LEVEE. Levee got to be Levee! And he don't need nobody messing with him about the white man – 'cause you don't know nothing about me. You don't know Levee. You don't know nothing about what kind of blood I got! What kind of heart I got beating here! I was eight years old when I watched a gang of white mens come into my daddy's house and have to do with my mama anyway they wanted. Never will forget it.

We was living in Jefferson County, about eighty miles outside of Natchez. My daddy's name was Memphis ... Memphis Lee Green ... had him near fifty acres of good farming land. I'm talking good land! Grow anything you want! He done gone off of shares and bought this land from Mr. Hallie's widow-woman after he done passed on. Folks called him an uppity nigger 'cause he done saved and borrowed to where he could buy this land and be independent.

It was coming on planting time and my daddy went into Natchez to get him some seed and fertilizer. Called me, say, Levee, you the man of the house now. Take care of your mama while I'm gone. I wasn't but a little boy, eight years old.

My mama was frying up some chicken when them

mens come in that house. Must have been eight or nine of them. She was standing there frying that chicken and them mens come and took hold of her just like you take hold of a mule and make him do what you want. There was my mama with a gang of white mens. She tried to fight them off, but I could see where it wasn't gonna do her any good. I didn't know what they were doing to her ... but I figured whatever it was they may as well do to me, too. My daddy had a knife that he kept around there for hunting and working and what not. I knew where he kept it and I went and got it. I'm gonna show you how spooked up I was by the white man. I tried my dammedest to cut one of them's throat! I hit him on the shoulder with it. He reached back and grabbed hold of that knife and whacked me across the chest with it. That's what made them stop. They was scared I was gonna bleed to death. My mama wrapped a sheet around me and carried me two miles down to the Furlow place and they drove me up to Doc Albans. He was waiting on a calf to be born and said he ain't had time to see me. They carried me up to Miss Etta, the midwife, and she fixed me up.

My daddy came back and acted like he done accepted the facts of what happened. But he got the names of them white men from my mama. He found out who they was and then we announced we was moving out of the county. Said good-bye to everybody ... all the neighbors. My daddy went and smiled in the face of one of them crackers who had been with my mama.

Smiled in his face and sold him our land. We moved over with relations in Caldwell. He got us settled in and then he took off one day. I ain't never seen him since. He sneaked back hiding up in the woods, laying to get them eight or nine men.

He got four of them before they got him. They tracked

him down in the woods. Caught up with him, hung him and set him afire. My daddy wasn't spooked up by the white man. No sir! And that taught me how to handle them. I seen my daddy go up and grin in this cracker's face ... smile in his face and sell him his land. All the while he's planning how he's gonna get him and what he's gonna do to him. That taught me how to handle them. So you all just back up and leave Levee alone about the white man. I can smile and say "yessir" to whoever I please. I got my time coming to me. You all just leave Levee alone about the white man.

Act 2, Scene 2

Ma Rainey is the biggest blues singer of her
time, and yet her white producers treat her
with very little respect. Ma confides her expe-
riences with her band leader, Cutler.

MA RAINEY. Bessie what? Ain't nobody thinking about
Bessie. I taught Bessie. She ain't doing nothing but
imitating me. What I care about Bessie? I don't care
if she sell a million records. She got her people and I
got mine. I don't care what nobody else do. Ma was the
first and don't you forget it!

I been doing this a long time. Ever since I was a little
girl. I don't care what nobody else do. That's what gets
me so mad with Irvin. White folks try to be put out
with you all the time. Too cheap to buy me a Coca-Cola.
I lets them know it though. Ma don't stand for no shit.
Wanna take my voice and trap it in them fancy boxes
with all them buttons and dials ... and then too cheap
to buy me a Coca-Cola. And it don't cost but a nickle a
bottle.

They don't care nothing about me. All they want is my
voice. Well, I done learned that and they gonna treat
me like I want to be treated no matter how much it
hurt them. They back there now calling me all kinds
of names ... calling me everything but a child of God.
But they can't do nothing else. They ain't got what they
wanted yet. As soon as they get my voice down on them
recording machines, then it's just like if I'd be some
whore and they roll over and put their pants on. Ain't
got no use for me then. I know what I'm talking about.
You watch. Irvin right there with the rest of them. He
don't care nothing about me either. He been my manager for six years and the only time he had me in his
house was to sing for some of his white friends.

If you colored and can make them some money then you alright with them. Otherwise you just a dog in the alley. I done made this company more money from my records than all the other recording artists they got put together. And they wanna balk about how much this session is costing them.

I don't pay that kind of talk no mind.

Act 2, Scene 1

While the recording session is on hold, Ma Rainey talks to Cutler and Toledo about the power of the blues.

MA RAINEY. It sure done got quiet in here. I never could stand no silence. I always got to have some music going on in my head somewhere. It keeps things balanced. Music will do that. It fills things up. The more music you got in the world, the fuller it is.

White folks don't understand about the blues. They hear it come out, but they don't know how it got there. They don't understand that's life's way of talking. You don't sing to feel better. You sing 'cause that's a way of understanding life.

The blues help you get out of bed in the morning. You get up knowing you ain't alone. There's something else in the world. Something's been added by that song. This be an empty world without the blues. I take that emptiness and try to fill it up with something.

I ain't started the blues way of singing. The blues always been here. They say I started it ... but I didn't. I just helped it out. Filled up that empty space a little bit. That's all. But if they wanna call me Mother of the Blues, that's all right with me. It don't hurt none.

Act 2, Scene 1

Toledo explains he has been foolish about a woman before and shares the story of his unsuccessful marriage that went sour once his wife joined the church.

TOLEDO. Now, I married a woman. A good woman. To this day I can't say she wasn't a good woman. I can't say nothing bad about her. I married that woman with all the good graces and intentions of being hooked up and bound to her for the rest of my life. I was looking for her to put me in my grave.

But you see ... it ain't all the time what your intentions and wishes are. She went out and joined the church. Alright. There ain't nothing wrong with that. A good Christian woman going to church and wanna do right by her God. There ain't nothing wrong with that. But she got up there, got to seeing them good Christian mens and wondering why I ain't like that. Soon she figure she got a heathen on her hands. She figured she couldn't live like that. The church was more important than I was. So she left. Packed up one day and moved out. To this day I ain't never said another word to her. Come home one day and my house was empty! And I sat down and figured out that I was a fool not to see that she needed something that I wasn't giving her. Else she wouldn't have been up there at the church in the first place. I ain't blaming her. I just said it wasn't gonna happen to me again. So yeah, Toledo been a fool about a woman. That's part of making life.

Act 2, Scene 1

*In response to Cutler's story of a black rev-
erend who was tortured by a group of white
men, Levee angrily asks where God was
during this horrible event.*

LEVEE. What I wants to know is ... if he's a man of God ...
then where the hell was God when all of this was going
on? Why wasn't God looking out for him? Why didn't
God strike down them crackers with some of this light-
ning you talking about to me?

What I care about burning in hell? You talking like a
fool ... burning in hell. Why didn't God strike some of
them crackers down? Tell me that! That's the question!
Don't come telling me this burning in hell shit! He a
man of God ... why didn't God strike some of them
crackers down? I'll tell you why! I'll tell you the truth!
It's sitting out there as plain as day! 'Cause he a white
man's God. That's why! God ain't never listened to no
nigger's prayers. God take a nigger's prayers and throw
them in the garbage. God don't pay niggers no mind.
In fact, God hate niggers! Hate them with all the fury
in his heart. Jesus don't love you. Jesus hate your black
ass! Come talking that shit to me. Talking about burning in hell! God can kiss my ass.

THE PIANO LESSON

Act 1, Scene 1

Doaker, who has been working with the railroad for twenty-seven years, shares his philosophy about people traveling every which way.

DOAKER. Twenty-seven years. Now, I'll tell you something about the railroad. What I done learned after twenty-seven years. See, you got North. You got West. You look over here you got South. Over there you got East. Now, you can start from anywhere. Don't care where you at. You got to go one of them four ways. And whichever way you decide to go they got a railroad that will take you there. Now, that's something simple. You think anybody would be able to understand that. But you'd be surprised how many people trying to go North get on a train going West. They think the train's supposed to go where they going rather than where it's going.

Now, why people going? Their sister's sick. They leaving before they kill somebody ... and they sitting across from somebody who's leaving to keep from getting killed. They leaving 'cause they can't get satisfied. They going to meet someone. I wish I had a dollar for every time that someone wasn't at the station to meet them. I done seen that a lot. In between the time they sent the telegram and the time the person get there ... they done forgot all about them.

They got so many trains out there they have a hard time keeping them from running into each other. Got trains going every which away. Got people on all of them. Somebody going where somebody just left. If everybody stay in one place I believe this would be a better world. Now what I done learned after twenty-seven years of rail roading is this ... if the train stays on the track ... it's going to get where it's going. It might not be where you going. If it ain't, then all you got to do is sit and wait 'cause the train's coming back to get you. The train don't never stop. It'll come back every time.

Act 1, Scene 1

Avery runs an elevator, but has hopes to become a reverend. He recounts a dream to Boy Willie and Lymon that inspires him to start the Good Sheppard Church.

AVERY. Well, it come to me in a dream. See ... I was sitting out in this railroad yard watching the trains go by. The train stopped and these three hoboes got off. They told me they had come from Nazareth and was on their way to Jerusalem. They had three candles. They gave me one and told me to light it ... but to be careful that it didn't go out. Next thing I knew I was standing in front of this house. Something told me to go knock on the door. This old woman opened the door and said they had been waiting on me. Then she led me into this room. It was a big room and it was full of all kinds of different people. They looked like anybody else except they all had sheep heads and was making noise like sheep make. I heard somebody call my name. I looked around and there was these same three hoboes. They told me to take off my clothes and they give me a blue robe with gold thread. They washed my feet and combed my hair. Then they showed me these three doors and told me to pick one.

I went through one of them doors and that flame leapt off that candle and it seemed like my whole head caught fire. I looked around and there was four or five other men standing there with these same blue robes on. Then we heard a voice tell us to look out across this valley. We looked out and saw the valley was full of wolves. The voice told us that these sheep people that I had seen in the other room had to go over to the other side of this valley and somebody had to take them. Then I heard another voice say "Who shall I send?" Next thing I knew I said, "Here I am. Send me." That's

when I met Jesus. He say "If you go, I'll go with you."
Something told me to say, "Come on. Let's go." That's
when I woke up. My head still felt like it was on fire
... but I had a peace about myself that was hard to
explain. I knew right then that I had been filled with
the Holy Ghost and called to be a servant of the Lord.
It took me a while before I could accept that. But then
a lot of little ways God showed me that it was true. So I
became a preacher.

Act 1, Scene 2

Wining Boy, who is a traveling musician, shares his wisdom about the difference between the black man and the white man, which is the law will always be on the "white man" side.

WINING BOY. Ain't no difference as far as how somebody supposed to treat you. I agree with that. But I'll tell you the difference between the colored man and the white man. All right. Now you take and eat some berries. They taste real good to you. So you say I'm gonna go out and get me a whole pot of these berries and cook them up to make a pie or whatever. But you ain't looked to see them berries is sitting in the white fellow's yard. Ain't got no fence around them. You figure anybody want something they'd fence it in. All right. Now the white man come along and say that's my land. Therefore everything that grow on it belong to me. He tell the sheriff "I want you to put this nigger in jail as a warning to all the other niggers. Otherwise first thing you know these niggers have everything that belong to us."

All right. Now Mr. So and So, he sell the land to you. And he come to you and say, "John, you own the land. It's all yours now. But them is my berries. And come time to pick them I'm gonna send my boys over. You got the land ... but them berries, I'm gonna keep them. They mine." And he go and fix it with the law that them is his berries. Now that's the difference between the colored man and the white man. The colored man can't fix nothing with the law.

Act 1, Scene 2

Boy Willie asks his uncle to play the piano.
Wining Boy refuses, sharing his complicated
relationship with the instrument. Although it
has brought him success, the piano has been
a source of much pain.

WINING BOY. I give that piano up. That was the best thing that ever happened to me, getting rid of that piano. That piano got so big and I'm carrying it around on my back. I don't wish that on nobody. See, you think it's all fun being a recording star. Got to carrying that piano around and man did I get slow. Got just like molasses. The world just slipping by me and I'm walking around with that piano. All right. Now, there ain't but so many places you can go. Only so many road wide enough for you and that piano. And that piano get heavier and heavier. Go to a place and they find out you play piano, the first thing they want to do is give you a drink, find you a piano, and sit you right down. And that's where you gonna be for the next eight hours. They ain't gonna let you get up! Now, the first three or four years of that is fun. You can't get enough whiskey and you can't get enough women and you don't never get tired of playing that piano. But that only last so long. You look up one day and you hate the whiskey, and you hate the women, and you hate the piano. But that's all you got. You can't do nothing else. All you know how to do is play that piano. Now, who am I? Am I me? Or am I the piano player? Sometime it seem like the only thing to do is shoot the piano player 'cause he the cause of all the trouble I'm having.

Act 1, Scene 2

Boy Willie would like to sell the family piano to buy the same piece of land where his ancestors were slaves. He feels his father would understand why he would trade the piano for the possibility of a better future.

BOY WILLIE. Now, I'm gonna tell you the way I see it. The only thing that make that piano worth something is them carvings Papa Willie Boy put on there. That's what make it worth something. That was my great grandaddy. Papa Boy Charles brought that piano into the house. Now, I'm supposed to build on what they left me. You can't do nothing with that piano sitting up here in the house. That's just like if I let them watermelons sit out there and rot. I'd be a fool. All right now, if you say to me, Boy Willie, I'm using that piano. I give out lessons on it and that help me make my rent or whatever. Then that be something else. I'd have to go on and say, well, Berniece using that piano. She building on it. Let her go on and use it. I got to find another way to get Sutter's land. But Doaker say you ain't touched that piano the whole time it's been up here. So why you wanna stand in my way? See, you just looking at the sentimental value. See, that's good. That's all right. I take my hat off whenever somebody say my daddy's name. But I ain't gonna be no fool about no sentimental value. You can sit up here and look at the piano for the next hundred years and it's just gonna be a piano. You can't make more than that. Now I want to get Sutter's land with that piano. I get Sutter's land and I can go down and cash in the crop and get my seed. As long as I got the land and the seed then I'm all right. I can always get me a little something else. 'Cause that land give back to you. I can make me another crop and cash that in. I still got the land and the seed. But that piano don't put out nothing else. You ain't got nothing working for you. Now, the kind of man my daddy was he would have understood that. I'm sorry you can't see it that way. But that's why I'm gonna take that piano out of here and sell it.

Act 1, Scene 2

Boy Willie's sister, Berniece, will not allow him to sell the piano. Their family has had a very violent past with this instrument. Berniece has witnessed how much pain it caused her mother. She would like this cycle of violence to stop.

BERNIECE. You ain't taking that piano out of my house. Look at this piano. Look at it. Mama Ola polished this piano with her tears for seventeen years. For seventeen years she rubbed on it till her hands bled. Then she rubbed the blood in ... mixed it up with the rest of the blood on it. Every day that God breathed life into her body she rubbed and cleaned and polished and prayed over it. "Play something for me, Berniece. Play something for me, Berniece." Every day. "I cleaned it up for you, play something for me, Berniece." You always talking about your daddy but you ain't never stopped to look at what his foolishness cost your mama. Seventeen years' worth of cold nights and an empty bed. For what? For a piano? For a piece of wood? To get even with somebody? I look at you and you're all the same. You, Papa Boy Charles, Wining Boy, Doaker, Crawley ... you're all alike. All this thieving and killing and thieving and killing. And what it ever lead to? More killing and more thieving. I ain't never seen it come to nothing. People getting burned up. People getting shot. People falling down their wells. It don't never stop.

Act 2, Scene 1

*After selling Lymon a suit and some shoes,
Wining Boy privately relates his relationship
with Lymon's mother.*

WINING BOY. His daddy was the same way. I used to run
around with him. I know his mama too. Two strokes
back and I would have been his daddy! His daddy's
dead now ... but I got the nigger out of jail one time.
They was fixing to name him Daniel and walk him
through the Lion's Den. He got in a tussle with one
of them white fellows and the sheriff lit on him like
white on rice. That's how the whole thing come about
between me and Lymon's mama. She knew me and his
daddy used to run together and he got in jail and she
went down there and took the sheriff a hundred dollars. Don't get me to lying about where she got it from.
I don't know. The sheriff looked at that hundred dollars
and turned his nose up. Told her say, "That ain't gonna
do him no good. You got to put another hundred on
top of that." She come up there and got me where I was
playing at this saloon ... said she had all but fifty dollars
and asked me if I could help. Now the way I figured
it ... without that fifty dollars the sheriff was gonna
turn him over to Parchman. The sheriff turn him over
to Parchman it be three years before anybody see him
again. Now I'm gonna say it right ... I will give anybody
fifty dollars to keep them out of jail for three years. I
give her the fifty dollars and she told me to come over
to the house. I ain't asked her. I figure if she was nice
enough to invite me I ought to go. I ain't had to say a
word. She invited me over just as nice. Say "Why don't
you come over to the house?" She ain't had to say nothing else. Them words rolled off her tongue just as nice. I
went on down there and sat about three hours. Started
to leave and changed my mind. She grabbed hold to me

and say, "Baby, it's all night long." That was one of the shortest nights I have ever spent on this earth! I could have used another eight hours. Lymon's daddy didn't even say nothing to me when he got out. He just looked at me funny. He had a good notion something had happened between me an' her. L. D. Jackson.

Act 2, Scene 2

Berniece, who has received a marriage pro-
posal from Avery, speaks about why, in 1936,
a woman cannot define herself without a
man in her life.

BERNIECE. You trying to tell me a woman can't be nothing
without a man. But you all right, huh? You can just
walk out of here without me – a woman – and still be
a man. That's all right. Ain't nobody gonna ask you,
"Avery, who you got to love you?" That's all right for
you. But everybody gonna be worried about Berniece.
"How Berniece gonna take care of herself? How she
gonna raise that child without a man? Wonder what
she do with herself. How she gonna live like that?"
Everybody telling me I can't be a woman unless I got a
man. Well, you tell me, Avery – you know – how much
woman am I?

Act 2, Scene 2

Avery has urged Berniece to play the piano to show Boy Willie that she is putting it to good use. Berniece shares the haunted memories that the piano still holds for her. She is determined not to put that burden on her daughter, Maretha.

BERNIECE. I done told you I don't play on that piano. Ain't no need in you to keep talking this choir stuff. When my mamma died I shut the top on that piano and I ain't never opened it since. I was only playing it for her. When my daddy died seem like all her life went into that piano. She used to have me playing on it ... had Miss Eula come in and teach me ... say when I played it she could hear my daddy talking to her. I used to think them pictures came alive and walked through the house. Sometime late at night I could hear my mamma talking to them. I said that wasn't gonna happen to me. I don't play that piano 'cause I don't want to wake them spirits. They never be walking around in this house.

I got Maretha playing on it. Let her go on and be a schoolteacher or something. She don't have to carry all of that with her. She got a chance I didn't have. I ain't gonna burden her with that piano.

Act 2, Scene 5

Boy Willie tells how he is not afriad of death
after his sister Berniece tries to scare him.

BOY WILLIE. She trying to scare me. Hell, I ain't scared of dying. I look around and see people dying every day. You got to die to make room for somebody else. I had a dog that died. Wasn't nothing but a puppy. I picked it up and put it in a bag and carried it up there to Reverend C. L. Thompson's church. I carried it up there and prayed and asked Jesus to make it live like he did the man in the Bible. I prayed real hard. Knelt down and everything. Say ask in Jesus' name. Well, I must have called Jesus' name two hundred times. I called his name till my mouth got sore. I got up and looked in the bag and the dog still dead. It ain't moved a muscle! I say, "Well, ain't nothing precious." And then I went out and killed me a cat. That's when I discovered the power of death. See, a nigger that ain't afraid to die is the worse kind of nigger for the white man. He can't hold that power over you. That's what I learned when I killed that cat. I got the power of death too. I can command him. I can call him up. The white man don't like to see that. He don't like for you to stand up and look him square in the eye and say, "I got it too." Then he got to deal with you square up.

Act 2, Scene 5

Recognizing the difficulties of his life, Boy Willie speaks about the struggles a young black person has in this world.

BOY WILLIE. What I want to bring a child into this world for? Why I wanna bring somebody else into all this for? I'll tell you this ... If I was Rockefeller I'd have forty or fifty. I'd make one every day. 'Cause they gonna start out in life with all the advantages. I ain't got no advantages to offer nobody. Many is the time I looked at my daddy and seen him staring off at his hands. I got a little older I know what he was thinking. He sitting there saying, "I got these big old hands but what I'm gonna do with them? Best I can do is make a fifty-acre crop for Mr. Stovall. Got these big old hands capable of doing anything. I can take and build something with these hands. But where's the tools? All I got is these hands. Unless I go out here and kill me somebody and take what they got ... it's a long row to hoe for me to get something of my own. So what I'm gonna do with these big old hands? What would you do?"

See now ... if he had his own land he wouldn't have felt that way. If he had something under his feet that belonged to him he could stand up taller. That's what I'm talking about. Hell, the land is there for everybody. All you got to do is figure out how to get you a piece. Ain't no mystery to life. You just got to go out and meet it square on. If you got a piece of land you'll find everything else fall right into place. You can stand right up next to the white man and talk about the price of cotton ... the weather, and anything else you want to talk about. If you teach that girl that she living at the bottom of life, she's gonna grow up and hate you.

Act 2, Scene 5

In the midst of fighting over the piano, Berniece tells Boy Willie that he's at the bottom of life. But Boy Willie reveals his passionate will to succeed.

BOY WILLIE. See now ... I'll tell you something about me. I done strung along and strung along. Going this way and that. Whatever way would lead me to a moment of peace. That's all I want. To be as easy with everything. But I wasn't born to that. I was born to a time of fire. The world ain't wanted no part of me. I could see that since I was about seven. The world say it's better off without me. See, Berniece accept that. She trying to come up to where she can prove something to the world. Hell, the world a better place 'cause of me. I don't see it like Berniece. I got a heart that beats here and it beats just as loud as the next fellow's. Don't care if he black or white. Sometime it beats louder. When it beats louder, then everybody can hear it. Some people get scared of that. Like Berniece. Some people get scared to hear a nigger's heart beating. They think you ought to lay low with that heart. Make it beat quiet and go along with everything the way it is. But my mama ain't birthed me for nothing. So what I got to do? I got to mark my passing on the road. Just like you write on a tree, "Boy Willie was here."

That's all I'm trying to do with that piano. Trying to put my mark on the road. Like my daddy done. My heart say for me to sell that piano and get me some land so I can make a life for myself to live in my own way. Other than that I ain't thinking about nothing Berniece got to say.

SEVEN GUITARS

Act 1, Scene 2

After Floyd returns to Pittsburgh, Vera describes the pain he inflicted on her after he left to go to Chicago with another woman.

VERA. It wasn't nothing to you but it was something to me. To have you just up and walk out like that. What you think happened to me? Did you ever stop to ask yourself, "I wonder how Vera doing – I wonder how she feel?" I lay here every night in an empty bed. In an empty room. Where? Someplace special? Someplace where you had been? The same room you walked out of? The same bed you turned your back on? You give it up and you want it? What kind of sense does that make?

You had what you wanted and I didn't. That makes you special. You one of them special people who is supposed to have everything just the way they want it.

I wanted to be that for you, Floyd. I wanted to know where you was bruised at. So I could be a woman for you. So I could touch you there. So I could spread myself all over you and know that I was a woman. That I could give a man only those things a woman has to give. And he could be satisfied. How much woman you think it make you feel to know you can't satisfy a man?

So he could say, "Yes, Vera a woman." That's what you say but you never believed it. You never showed me all those places where you were a man. You went to Pearl Brown and you showed her. I don't know what she did or didn't do but I looked up and you was back here after I had given you up. After I had walked through an empty house for a year and a half looking for you. After I would lay myself out on that bed and search my body for your fingerprints. "He touched me here. Floyd touched me here and he touched me here and he

87

touched me here and he kissed me here and he gave me here and he took here and he ain't here he ain't here he ain't here quit looking for him 'cause he ain't here he's there! there! there! there!"

He's there. In Chicago with another woman and all I have is a little bit of nothing, a little bit of touching, a little bit of myself left. It ain't even here no more what you looking for. What you remember. It ain't even here no more.

Act 1, Scene 4

Louise is warning her friend Vera about trusting men. She tells her that Floyd reminds her of Henry, the last man she allowed herself to love.

LOUISE. However it go he make it go that way. He remind me of Henry. That man walked out on me and that was the best thing that happened to me. When he left I told myself say, "If you have to say hello before you can say good-bye I ain't never got to worry about nobody saying good-bye to me no more." I ain't never going through one of them good-byes again. He was standing upstairs in the hallway. Told me say, "I'm leaving." I asked him, "What for? After twelve years. Why you gonna leave after all this time? After you done used me up." He say, "It's something I got to do." Then he went on and gathered up his things. He left a razor and a pair of shoes. They still up there.

He got to the doorway and I told him, "Leave your pistol. Don't leave me here by myself." He ain't said nothing. He took out his pistol and handed it to me. I told him say, "I ought to shoot you." We laughed and then he kissed me good-bye. I ain't seen him since. I got that pistol upstairs now. What I'm trying to tell you is, don't let no man use you up and talk about he gotta go. Shoot him first.

Act 1, Scene 4

*While setting up a card table, the men com-
pare the women in their lives. Red Carter tells
them he once had a different woman for every
day of the week.*

RED CARTER. Where they at. I know how to handle them. I
used to have seven women. I tried to keep them separate and give them all a day of the week. But that didn't
work. I told one of them, "I'll see you on Tuesday. I
got something to do Monday." She say, "Naw, Naw ...
I see you Friday night." I told the other one, "I'll see
you on Thursday I got something to do Tuesday." She
say, "Naw, Naw ... I'll see you Friday." They all wanted
to see me on Friday 'cause I was working. There was
a time I couldn't get a woman. I go anywhere near
a woman they get up and run. Time I got me a job I
couldn't keep them off me. Women everywhere. All of a
sudden I got right popular ... except they all wanna see
me on Friday. I tried to move my Friday woman over to
Sunday but she got mad. My Sunday woman quit me
and my Monday woman wanted to see me on Saturday.
I got so confused I say the best thing for me to do was
quit my job.

Act 2, Scene 1

Hedley shares the story of how he got his name. He believes that he could someday be the father of the man who will lead the black man out of bondage.

HEDLEY. My father play the trumpet and for him Buddy Bolden was a God. He was in New Orleans with the boats when he make them run back and forth from Haiti to New Orleans. The trumpet was his first love. He never forgot that night he heard Buddy Bolden play. Sometime he talked about it. He drink his rum, play his trumpet, and if you were lucky that night he would talk about Buddy Bolden. I say lucky 'cause you never see him like that with his face light up and something be driving him from inside and it was a thing he love more than my mother. That is how he names me, King ... after King Buddy Bolden. It is not a good thing he named me that. *(Pause.)* I killed a man once. A black man. I am not sorry I killed him.

He would not call me King. He laughed to think a black man could be King. I did not want to lose my name so I told him to call me the name my father give me and he laugh. He would not call me King and I beat him hard with a stick. That is what cost me my time with a woman. After that I don't tell nobody my name is King. It is a bad thing. Everybody say Hedley crazy 'cause he black. 'Cause he know the place of the black man is not at the foot of the white man's boot. Maybe it is not alright in my head sometimes. 'Cause I don't like the world. I don't like what I see from the people. The people is too small. I always want to be a big man. Like Jesus Christ was a big man. He was the son of the Father. I too. I am the son of my father. Maybe Hedley never going to be big like that. But for himself inside. That place where you live your own special life. I would be happy to be big there. And maybe my child, if it be a boy, he would be big like Moses. I think about that. Somebody have to be the father of the man to lead the black man out of bondage. Marcus Garvey have a father. Maybe if I could not be like Marcus Garvey then I could be the father of someone who would not bow down to the white man. Maybe I could be the father of the messiah. I am fifty-nine years old and my times is running out. Hedley is looking for a woman to lie down with and make his first baby. Maybe ... maybe you be that woman for me. Maybe we both be blessed.

Act 2, Scene 2

Ruby has come to Pittsburgh to escape a romantic tragedy she experienced in the South.

RUBY. I ain't done nothing to make him jealous. He was always like that. He was jealous when I met him. He don't know that just make you wanna leave him quicker. He trying to hold onto you and end up driving you away. Elmore started to get mean so I left him. Everybody seen me and Leroy together and knew I had quit Elmore. I told Leroy Elmore was jealous of him. He say he didn't care. Say he still loved me. Asked me who did I love. I told him the truth. I didn't love neither one of them. They both was nice in their own way. Then they got into a fight. I tried to tell them Ruby don't belong to nobody and Ruby ain't gonna take but so much of anybody. After the fight I saw Elmore and he asked me where Leroy was. Say he wanted to go make up. I told him Leroy was at the barber shop and he went up there and shot him before Leroy could have a chance to say anything. The problem with Elmore was he never could get enough of me. He used to tell me he wanted to take it all so nobody else could have me. He wasn't gonna leave none for nobody else to hear him tell it. That make you feel funny to be with a man want to use you up like that.

Act 2, Scene 3

Floyd has just learned that his manager got arrested for selling fake insurance. He makes the declaration that even if every opportunity is taken away from him, these setbacks will not stop him from going to Chicago to make another record.

FLOYD. I had seven ways to go. They cut that down to six. I say let me try one of them six. They cut it down to five. Everytime I push ... they pull. They cut it down to four. I say what's the matter? Everything can't go wrong all the time. They cut it down to three. I say three is better than two. I really don't need but one. They cut it down to two. See ... I'm going to Chicago. If I have to buy me a graveyard and kill everybody I see. I am going to Chicago. I don't want to live my life without. Everybody I know live without. I don't want to do that. I want to live with. I don't know what you all think of yourself but I think I'm supposed to have. Whatever it is. Have something. Have anything. My mama lived and died she ain't had nothing. If it ain't nothing but peace of mind then let me have that. My mama ain't had two dimes to rub together. And ain't had but one stick. She got to do without the fire. Some kind of warmth in her life. I don't want to live in a cold house. It's a cold world let me have a little shelter from it. That's all I want. Floyd Barton is gonna make his record. Floyd Barton is going to Chicago.

Act 2, Scene 4

*Hedley wants to fight the white man the same
way Toussaint L'Ouverture (a revolutionary
hero from his native Haiti) fought for libera-
tion. He keeps a machete hidden until the end
of the monologue.*

HEDLEY. Where? Oh this? When I was a little boy I learn
about Toussaint L'Ouverture in the school. Miss
Manning. She say listen you little black-as-sin niggers,
you never each and none of you amount to nothing,
you grow up to cut the white man cane and your whole
life you never can be nothing as God is my witness,
but I will tell you of a black boy who was a man and
made the white man run from the blood in the street.
Like that you know. Then she tell us about Toussaint
L'Ouverture. I say I going to be just like that. Everybody
say that you know. I go home and my daddy he sitting
there and he big and black and tired taking care of the
white man's horses and I say how come you not like
Toussaint L'Ouverture why you do nothing? And he
kick me with him boot in my mouth. I shut up that day
you know and then when Marcus Garvey come he give
me back my voice to speak. It was on my father's death
bed, with Death standing there I say to him, "Father, I
sorry about Toussaint L'Ouverture, Miss Manning say
nobody ever amount to nothing and I never did again
try. Then Marcus Garvey come and say that it was not
true and that she lied and I forgive you kick me and I
hope as God is with us now but a short time more that
you forgive me my tongue." It was hard to say these
things but I confess my love for my father and Death
standing there say, "I already took him a half hour ago."
And he cold as a boot, cold as a stone and hard like
iron. I cried a river of tears but he was too heavy to
float on them. So I dragged him with me these years

across an ocean. Then my father come to me in a dream
and say he was sorry he died without forgiving me my
tongue and that he would send Buddy Bolden with
some money for me to buy a plantation. Then I get the
letter from the white man who come to take me away.
So I say, Hedley, be smart, go and see Joe Roberts. We
sat and talked man to man. Joe Roberts is a nice man.
I told him about Toussaint L'Ouverture and my father
and Joe Roberts smile and he say he had something to
give me. And he give to me this. Now Hedley ready for
the white man when he come to take him away.

Act 2, Scene 6

*Floyd has just proposed marriage to Vera
and asks her to join him in Chicago. When
she resists, he explains why he left with Pearl
Brown years before, and why he needs her
now.*

FLOYD. You was there too, Vera. You had a hand in whatever it was. Maybe all the times we don't know the
effect of what we do. But we cause what happens to
us. Sometimes even in little ways we can't see. I went
up to Chicago with Pearl Brown 'cause she was willing
to believe that I could take her someplace she wanted
to go. That I could give her things that she wanted to
have. She told me by that ... it was possible. Even sometimes when you question yourself ... when you wonder
can you really make the music work for you ... can you
find a way to get it out into the world so it can burst
in the air and have it mean something to somebody.
She didn't know if I could do that. If I could have a
hit record. But she was willing to believe it. Maybe it
was selfish of her. Maybe she believed for all the wrong
reasons. But that gave me a chance to try. So yeah ...
I took it. It wasn't easy. I was scared. But when them
red lights came on in that recording studio it was like a
bell ringing in the boxing match and I did it! I reached
down inside me and I pulled out whatever was there.
I did like my mama told me. I did my best. And I figured nobody could fault me for that. Then when they
didn't release the record, Pearl Brown left. She thought
she had believed wrong. I don't fault her for that. But I
never lost the belief in myself. Then when they released
the record I realized I didn't have nothing but a hit
record. I come back to you figuring you couldn't say no

to a man who got a hit record. But you did. And that
made me see that you wanted more than Pearl Brown.
I'm here saying I can give it to you. Try me one more
time and I'll never jump back on you in life.

Act 2, Scene 7

*Louise is waiting for everyone to get dressed
to go to the Mother's Day dance. As she waits
she reflects on the recent comings and goings
in her back yard.*

LOUISE. I know it don't take all day to get dressed. I'm
dressed. Seem like everybody should be dressed. My
mother used to tell me I was gonna be late for my own
funeral. She might be right. But then I won't have to
worry about getting a seat. I don't know if I can take it
no more. They about to drive me crazy. The House of
Blues, the Blue Goose, the Red Carter, the dead rooster,
the this-that-and-the-other, hurry up and sit down and
let's dance and give me a drink and what I got? Who
ain't don't know where the other one is or went or ain't
going or is going and this one's dead and that one's
dying and who shot who and who sung what song and
give me another drink and here go a dollar and I ain't
got a dime and what's the use and who to do and where
ain't you been 'cause being ain't no telling.

Act 2, Scene 7

*While Floyd was in Chicago, Vera and
Canewell were involved. Vera reveals that she
is going to marry Floyd. Canewell responds
with tenderness as he shares his thoughts on
love.*

CANEWELL. I always did believe in love. I felt like if you don't
believe in love you may as well not believe in nothing.
Even love that ain't but halfway is still love. And that
don't make it no less 'cause it's only coming one way.
If it was two ways it still be the same amount of love.
Just like say I loved you and you didn't love me back.
I can still say I'm all filled up with love for Vera. I go
walking down the street people can see that. They don't
know what to call it but they can see something going
on. Maybe they see a man who look like he satisfied
with life and that make him walk more better. Make
him walk like he got a million dollars in his pocket. If
I loved you and this time you loved me back. I don't
see where my love for you can get more bigger that it
already was. Unless I walk like I got two million dollars. Sometime people don't count it if you ain't loved
back. But I count it all the same. Some women make
their bed up so high don't nobody know how to get to
it. I know you ain't like that. You know how to make
your bed up high and turn you lamp down low. That's
why Floyd don't want to lose you. I think you and Floyd
ought to go ahead and see what you all can make of it.

FENCES

Act 1, Scene 1

*During the Friday night ritual of sharing a
pint of gin with his best friend Bono, Troy
spins an elaborate story of his battle with
Death.*

TROY. Death ain't nothing. I done seen him. Done wrassled
with him. You can't tell me nothing about death. Death
ain't nothing but a fastball on the outside corner. And
you know what I'll do to that! You get one of them fast-
balls, about waist high over the outside corner of the
plate where you can get the meat of the ball on it ... and
good God! You can kiss it goodbye.

I looked up one day and Death was marching straight
at me. Like soldiers on parade! The Army of Death was
marching straight at me. The middle of July, 1941. It
got real cold just like it be winter. It seem like Death
himself reached out and touched me on the shoulder.
He touch me just like I touch you. I got cold as ice and
Death standing there grinning at me.

I say ... "What you want, Mr. Death? You be wanting
me? You done brought your army to be getting me?" I
looked him dead in the eye. I wasn't fearing nothing. I
was ready to tangle. Just like I'm ready to tangle now.
The Bible say be ever vigilant.

Death standing there staring at me ... carrying that
sickle in his hand. Finally he say, "You want bound
over for another year?" See, just like that ... "You want
bound over for another year?" I told him, "Bound over
hell! Let's settle this now!" It seem like he kinda fell
back when I said that, and all the cold went out of me.
I reached down and grabbed that sickle and threw it
just as far as I could throw it ... and me and him commenced to wrestling.

We wrestled for three days and three nights. I can't say where I found the strength from. Everytime it seem like he was gonna get the best of me, I'd reach way down deep inside myself and find the strength to do him one better.

All right. At the end of the third night we done weakened each other to where we can't hardly move. Death stood up, throwed on his robe ... had him a white robe with a hood on it. He throwed on that robe and went off to look for his sickle. Say, "I'll be back." Just like that. "I'll be back." I told him say, "Yeah, but ... you gone have to find me!" I wasn't no fool. I wasn't going looking for him. Death ain't nothing to play with. And I know he's gonna get me. I know I got to join his army ... his camp followers. But as long as I keep my strength and see him coming ... as long as I keep my vigilance ... he's gonna have to fight to get me. I ain't going easy.

Act 1, Scene 1

Troy's son, Lyons, drops by to borrow ten dollars. Instead of giving him the money, Troy tells a story about getting in debt with the devil.

TROY. Look here, Bono ... I went down to see Hertzberger about some furniture. Got three rooms for two-ninety-eight. That what it say on the radio. "Three rooms ... two-nincty-eight." Even made up a little song about it. Go down there ... man tell me I can't get no credit. I'm working every day and can't get no credit. What to do? I got an empty house with some raggedy furniture in it. Cory ain't got no bed. He's sleeping on a pile of rags on the floor. Working every day and can't get no credit. Come back here – Rose'll tell you – madder than hell. Sit down ... try to figure what I'm gonna do. Come a knock on the door. Ain't been living here but three days. Who know I'm here? Open the door ... devil standing there bigger than life. White fellow ... go on good clothes and everything. Standing there with a clipboard in his hand. I ain't had to say nothing. First words come out of his mouth was ... "I understand you need some furniture and can't get no credit." I liked to fell over. He say, "I'll give you all the credit you want, but you got to pay the interest on it." I told him, "Give me three rooms' worth and charge whatever you want." Next day a truck pulled up here and two men unloaded them three rooms. Man what drove the truck give me a book. Say send ten dollars, first of every month to the address in the book and everything will be all right. Say if I miss a payment the devil was coming back and it'll be hell to pay. That was fifteen years ago. To this day ... the first of the month I send my ten dollars, Rose'll tell you.

I ain't never seen that man since. Now you tell me who

else that could have been but the devil? I ain't sold
my soul or nothing like that, you understand. Naw, I
wouldn't have truck with the devil about nothing like
that. I got my furniture and pays my ten dollars the
first of the month just like clockwork.

Act 1, Scene 3

When Cory has asked his father why he doesn't like him, Troy tells him that responsibility and respect are more important than being liked.

TROY. Like you? I go out of here every morning ... bust my butt ... putting up with them crackers every day ... 'cause I like you? You about the biggest fool I ever saw. *(Pause.)* It's my job. It's my responsibility! You understand that? A man got to take care of his family. You live in my house ... sleep in you behind on my bed-clothes ... fill you belly up with my food ... 'cause you my son. You my flesh and blood. Not 'cause I like you! 'Cause it's my duty to take care of you. I owe a responsibility to you!

Let's get this straight right here ... before it go along any further ... I ain't got to like you. Mr. Rand don't give me my money come payday 'cause he likes me. He gives me 'cause he owe me. I don't give you everything I had to give you. I gave you your life! Me and your mama worked that out between us. And liking your black ass wasn't part of the bargain. Don't you try and go through life worrying about if somebody like you or not. You best be making sure they doing right by you. You understand what I'm saying, boy?

Then get the hell out of my face, and get on down to that A&P.

Act 1, Scene 4

*As Bono and Lyons chat about their fathers,
Troy describes a figure who fulfilled his
responsibilities, but was an evil man.*

TROY. My daddy ain't had them walking blues! What you
talking about? He stayed right there with his family. But
he was just as evil as he could be. My mama couldn't
stand him. Couldn't stand that evilness. She run off
when I was about eight. She sneaked off one night after
he had gone to sleep. Told me she was coming back
for me. I ain't never seen her no more. All his women
run off and left him. He wasn't good for nobody. When
my turn come to head out, I was fourteen and got to
sniffing around Joe Canewell's daughter. Had us an
old mule we called Greyboy. My daddy sent me out to
do some plowing and I tied up Greyboy and went to
fooling around with Joe Canewell's daughter. We done
found us a nice little spot, got real cozy with each other.
She about thirteen and we done figured we was grown
anyway ... so we down there enjoying ourselves ... ain't
thinking about nothing. We didn't know Greyboy had
got loose and wandered back to the house and my daddy
was looking for me. We down there by the creek enjoying ourselves when my daddy come up on us. Surprised
us. He had them leather straps off the mule and commenced to whopping me like there was no tomorrow.
I jumped up, mad and embarrassed. I was scared of
my daddy. When he commenced to whopping on me ...
quite naturally I run to get out of the way. *(Pause.)* Now
I thought he was mad 'cause I ain't done my work. But
I see where he was chasing me off so he could have the
gal for himself. When I see what the matter of it was, I
lost all fear of my daddy. Right there is where I become
a man ... at fourteen years of age. *(Pause.)* Now it was
my turn to run him off. I picked up them same reins

that he had used on me. I picked up them reins and commenced to whopping on him. The gal jumped up and run off ... and when my daddy turned to face me, I could see why the devil had never come to get him ... 'cause he was the devil himself. I don't know what happened. When I woke up, I was laying right there by the creek, and Blue ... this old dog we had ... was licking my face. I thought I was blind. I couldn't see nothing. Both my eyes were swollen shut. I layed there and cried. I didn't know what I was gonna do. The only thing I knew was the time had come for me to leave my daddy's house. And right there the world suddenly got big. And it was a long time before I could cut it down to where I could handle it. Part of that cutting down was when I got to the place where I could feel him kicking in my blood and knew that the only thing that separated us was the matter of a few years.

Act 1, Scene 4

Troy tells of leaving his father's house at four-teen years old and the difficulties of being a young man in the city with no skills and no possibilities for living an honest life.

TROY. I walked on down to Mobile and hitched up with some of them fellows that was heading this way. Got up here and found out ... not only couldn't you get a job ... you couldn't find no place to live. I thought I was in freedom. Shhh. Colored folks living down there on the riverbanks in whatever kind of shelter they could find for themselves. Right down there under the Brady Street Bridge. Living in shacks made of sticks and tar paper. Messed around there and went from bad to worse. Started stealing. First it was food. Then I figured, hell, if I steal money I can buy me some food. Buy me some shoes too! One thing led to another. Met your mama. I was young and anxious to be a man. Met your mama and had you. What I do that for? Now I got to worry about feeding you and her. Got to steal three times as much. Went out one day looking for somebody to rob ... that's what I was, a robber. I'll tell you the truth. I'm ashamed of it today. But it's the truth. Went to rob this fellow ... pulled out my knife ... and he pulled out a gun. Shot me in the chest. It felt just like somebody had taken a hot branding iron and laid it on me. When he shot me I jumped at him with my knife. They told me I killed him and they put me in the penitentiary and locked me up for fifteen years. That's where I met Bono. That's where I learned how to play baseball. Got out that place and your mama had taken you and went on to make life without me. Fifteen years was a long time for her to wait. But that fifteen years cured me of that robbing stuff. Rose'll tell you. She asked me when I met her if I had gotten all that foolishness out of my system. And I told her, "Baby, it's you and baseball all what count with me." You hear me, Bono? I meant it too. She say, "Which one comes first?" I told her, "Baby, ain't no doubt it's baseball ... but you stick and get old with me and we'll both outlive this baseball." Am I right, Rose? And it's true.

Act 2, Scene 1

As Troy reveals to Rose that he will be the father of another woman's baby, he tries to justify his actions by sharing his need to get more out of life.

TROY. Rose, I done tried all my life to live decent ... to live a clean ... hard ... useful life. I tried to be a good husband to you. In every way I knew how. Maybe I come into the world backwards, I don't know. But ... you born with two strikes on you before you come to the plate. You got to guard it closely ... always looking for the curveball on the inside corner. You can't afford to let none get past you. You can't afford a call strike. If you going down ... you going down swinging. Everything lined up against you. What you gonna do. I fooled them, Rose. I bunted. When I found you and Cory and a halfway decent job ... I was safe. Couldn't nothing touch me. I wasn't gonna strike out no more. I wasn't going back to the penitentiary. I wasn't gonna lay in the streets with a bottle of wine. I was safe. I had me a family. A job. I wasn't gonna get that last strike. I was on first looking for one of them boys to knock me in. To get me home.

Then when I saw that girl ... she firmed up my backbone. And I got to thinking that if I tried ... I just might be able to steal second. Do you understand, after eighteen years I wanted to steal second.

Act 2, Scene 1

*In response to Troy's revelation, Rose, heart-
broken, speaks up about the sacrifices she has
had to make in their marriage. She has had
to put aside many parts of herself to make a
life and family with Troy, and it has not been
easy.*

ROSE. I been standing with you! I been right here with you,
Troy. I got a life too. I gave eighteen years of my life
to stand in the same spot with you. Don't you think
I ever wanted other things? Don't you think I had
dreams and hopes? What about my life? What about
me. Don't you think it ever crossed my mind to want to
know other men? That I wanted to lay up somewhere
and forget about my responsibilities? That I wanted
someone to make me laugh so I could feel good? You
not the only one who's got wants and needs. But I held
on to you, Troy. I took all my feelings, my wants and
needs, my dreams ... and I buried them inside you. I
planted a seed and waited and prayed over it. I planted
myself inside you and waited to bloom. And it didn't
take me no eighteen years to find out the soil was hard
and rocky and it wasn't never gonna bloom. But I held
on to you, Troy, I held you tighter. You was my husband. I owed you everything I had. Every part of me
I could find to give you. And upstairs in that room ...
with the darkness falling in on me ... I gave everything
I had to try and erase the doubt that you wasn't the
finest man in the world, and wherever you was going ...
I wanted to be there with you. 'Cause you was my husband. 'Cause that's the only way I was gonna survive as
your wife. You always talking about what you give ...
and what you don't have to give. But you take too. You
take ... and don't even know nobody's giving!

Act 2, Scene 5

Cory left his father's house eight years ago and joined the Marines. Returning home for the first time after hearing about Troy's death, he tells Rose why he cannot go to the funeral.

CORY. The whole time I was growing up ... living in his house ... Papa was like a shadow that followed you everywhere. It weighed on you and sunk into your flesh. It would wrap around you and lay there until you couldn't tell which one was you anymore. That shadow digging in your flesh. Trying to crawl in. Trying to live through you. Everywhere I looked, Troy Maxson was staring back at me ... hiding under the bed ... in the closet. I'm just saying I've got to find a way to get rid of that shadow, Mama.

I don't want to be Troy Maxson. I want to be me.

Act 2, Scene 5

When Cory tells Rose that he isn't going to
Troy's funeral, Rose reflects on her life with
her husband and forgives Troy for all his
faults.

ROSE. You can't be nobody but who you are, Cory. That
shadow wasn't nothing but you growing into yourself.
You either got to grow into it or cut it down to fit you.
But that's all you got to make life with. That's all you
got to measure yourself against that world out there.
Your daddy wanted you to be everything he wasn't ...
and at the same time he tried to make you into everything he was. I don't know if he was right or wrong
... but I do know he meant to do more good than he
meant to do harm. He wasn't always right. Sometimes
when he touched he bruised. And sometimes when
he took me in his arms he cut. When I first met your
daddy I thought ... Here is a man I can lay down with
and make a baby. That's the first thing I thought when
I seen him. I was thirty years old and had done seen my
share of men. But when he walked up to me and said,
"I can dance a waltz that'll make you dizzy," I thought,
Rose Lee, here is a man that you can open yourself up
to and be filled to bursting. Here is a man that can fill
all them empty spaces you been tipping around the
edges of. One of them empty spaces was being somebody's mother. I married your daddy and settled down
to cooking his supper and keeping clean sheets on the
bed. When your daddy walked through the house he
was so big he filled it up. That was my first mistake.
Not to make him leave some room for me. For my part
in the matter. But at that time I wanted that. I wanted
a house that I could sing in. And that's what your daddy
gave me. I didn't know to keep up his strength I had to
give up little pieces of mine. I did that. I took on his life

as mine and mixed up the pieces so that you couldn't hardly tell which was which anymore. It was my choice. It was my life and I didn't have to live it like that. But that's what life offered me in the way of being a woman and I took it. I grabbed hold of it with both hands. By the time Raynell came into the house, me and your daddy had done lost touch with one another. I didn't want to make my blessing off of nobody's misfortune ... but I took on to Raynell like she was all them babies I had wanted and never had. Like I'd been blessed to relive a part of my life. And if the Lord see fit to keep up my strength ... I'm gonna do her just like your daddy did you ... I'm gonna give her the best of what's in me ...

TWO TRAINS
RUNNING

Act 1, Scene 1

Memphis sees his neighborhood going downhill, everyone is suffering except the undertaker. As the city is purchasing his property for redevelopment, he announces that he deserves to be justly compensated.

MEMPHIS. Ain't nothing to do. Unless I do like West and go into the undertaking business. I can't go out there in Squirrel Hill and open up a restaurant. Ain't nothing gonna be left around here. Supermarket gone. Two drugstores. The five and ten. Doctor done moved out. Dentist done moved out. Shoe store gone. Ain't nothing gonna be left but these niggers killing one another. That don't never go out of style. West gonna get richer and everybody else gonna get poorer. At one time you couldn't get a seat in here. Had the jukebox working and everything. Time somebody get up somebody sit down before they could get out the door. People coming from everywhere. Everybody got to eat and everybody got to sleep. Some people don't have stoves. Some people don't have nobody to cook for them. Men whose wives done died and left them. Cook for them thirty years and lay down and die. Who's gonna cook for them now? Somebody got to do it. I order four cases of chicken on Friday and Sunday it's gone. Fry it up. Make a stew. Boil it. Add some dumplings. You couldn't charge more than a dollar. But then you didn't have to. It didn't cost you but a quarter. People used to come from all over. The man used to come twice a week to collect the jukebox. He making more money than I am. He pay seventy-five cents for the record and he make two hundred dollars off it. If it's a big hit he's liable to make four hundred. The record will take all the quarters you can give it. It don't never wear out. The chicken be gone by Sunday. It ain't nothing like that now. I'm lucky if I go through a case a chicken a week. That's all right. I'll take that. I ain't greedy. But if they wanna tear it down they gonna have to meet my price.

Act 1, Scene 2

Memphis learns that Sterling quit his job working construction and calls black men "lazy". Holloway vehemently disagrees and argues that if it weren't for the black labor force, white America would not have the wealth it has now.

HOLLOWAY. People kill me talking about niggers is lazy. Niggers is the most hardworking people in the world. Worked three hundred years for free. And didn't take no lunch hour. Now all of a sudden niggers is lazy. Don't know how to work. All of a sudden when they got to pay niggers, ain't no work for him to do. If it wasn't for you the white man would be poor. Every little bit he got he got standing on top of you. That's why he could reach so high. He give you three dollars a day for six months and he got him a railroad for the next hundred years. All you got is six months' worth of three dollars a day.

Now you can't even get that. Ain't no money in niggers working. Look out there on the street. If there was some money in it ... if the white man could figure out a way to make some money by putting niggers to work ... we'd all be working. He ain't building no more railroads. He got them. He ain't building no more highways. Somebody done already stuck the telephone poles in the ground. That's been done already. The white man ain't stacking no more niggers. You know what I'm talking about, stacking niggers, don't you? Well, here's how that go. If you ain't got nothing ... you can go out here and get you a nigger. Then you got something, see. You got one nigger. If that one nigger get out there and plant something ... get something out the ground ... even if it ain't nothing but a bushel of potatoes ... then you got one nigger and one bushel of potatoes. Then you take that bushel of potatoes and go get you another nigger. Then you got two niggers. Put them to work and you got two niggers and two bushels of potatoes. See, now you can go buy two more niggers. That's how you stack a nigger on top of a nigger. White folks got to stacking ... and I'm talking about they stacked up some niggers! Stacked up close to fifty million niggers. If you stacked them on top of one another they make six or seven circles around the moon. It's lucky the boat didn't sink with all them niggers they had stacked up there. It take them two extra months to get here 'cause it ride so low in the water. They couldn't find you enough work back then. Now that they got to pay you they can't find you none. If this was different time wouldn't be nobody out there on the street. They'd all be in the cotton fields.

Act 1, Scene 2

*Sterling invites everyone in the restaurant
to come to a rally in honor of Malcolm X's
birthday. Memphis is not in agreement with
the promise of political change offered by the
Black Power Movement.*

MEMPHIS. That's what half the problem is ... these Black
Power niggers. They got people confused. They don't
know what they doing themselves. These niggers talking about freedom, justice and equality and don't know
what it mean. You born free. It's up to you to maintain
it. You born with dignity and everything else. These
niggers talking about freedom, but what you gonna do
with it? Freedom is heavy. You got to put your shoulder to freedom. Put your shoulder to it and hope your
back hold up. And if you around here looking for justice, you got a long wait. Ain't no justice. That's why
they got that statue of her and got her blindfolded.
Common sense would tell you if anybody need to see
she do. There ain't no justice. Jesus Christ didn't get
justice. What makes you think you gonna get it? That's
just the nature of the world. These niggers talking
about they want freedom, justice and equality. Equal
to what? Hell, I might be a better man than you. What
I look like going around here talking about I want to
be equal to you? I don't know how these niggers think
sometimes. Talking about black power with their hands
and their pockets empty. You can't do nothing without
a gun. Not in this day and time. That's the only kind
of power the white man understand. They think they
gonna talk their way up on it. In order to talk your way
you got to have something under the table. These niggers don't understand that. If I tell you to get out my
yard and leave my apples alone, I can't talk you out.
You sit up in the tree and laugh at me. But if you know

I might come out with a shotgun ... that be something different. You'd have to think twice about whether you wanted some apples. These niggers around here talking about they black and beautiful. Sound like they trying to convince themselves. You got to think you ugly to run around shouting you beautiful. You don't hear me say that. Hell, I know I look nice. Got good manners and everything.

Act 2, Scene 1

*West, the undertaker, has buried a lot of
people, but the most tragic was the burial of
his beloved wife. In order to find out if his
wife is in heaven, West goes to see Aunt Ester.*

WEST. I went up there to see if my wife was in heaven. I done
buried a whole lot of people, but she the first one I ever
wondered about. See, people don't understand about
death, but if you ever hear one of them coffin sounds
you'd know. There ain't nothing like it. That coffin get
to talking and you know that this here ... this what we
call life ain't nothing. You can blow it away with a blink
of an eye. But death ... you can't blow away death. It
lasts forever. I didn't understand about it till my wife
died. Before that it was just a job. Then when she died
I come to understand it. You can live to be a hundred
and fifty and you'll never have a greater moment than
when you breathe your last breath. Ain't nothing you
can do in life compared to it. See, right then you done
something. You became a part of everything that come
before. And that's a great thing. Ain't nothing you can
do in life compared to that. So I heard about Aunt
Ester and went to see if my wife was in heaven. I figure
if anybody know she would.

She told me to take and throw twenty-five dollars in
the river and come back and see her. I thought she was
crazy, to tell you the truth. I didn't pay her no mind. I
knew she was old, but I figured she had gotten too old.

I offered to give her twenty-five dollars just for her
time ... but she wouldn't take it. Told me to throw it in
the river. I'd rather see her with it than to see it at the
bottom of the river. I just wasn't gonna do that with my
money.

Act 1, Scene 3

*Memphis shoots down the idea of burning
down the restaurant to claim the insurance
money. He makes a proclamation that he will
not make any more compromises in his life,
and that he will stand his ground in the sale
of his restaurant.*

MEMPHIS. Nigger, is you crazy! Insurance cost five times
what the building is worth. That's why I keep me some
good tenants upstairs. I don't put none of them fools
up there that's liable to get drunk and burn down the
place. When Mr. Collins died I let it set empty three
months till I got somebody up there that was responsible. Look back in the kitchen ... ask Risa ... I got four
or five fire extinguishers back there ... and you talking
about burning down the place. That's the one thing
I am scared of. If it burn down I don't get nothing. I
don't even get the fifteen thousand. See, they don't
know. The half ain't never been told. I'm ready to walk
through fire. I don't bother nobody. The last person
I bothered is dead. My mama died in '54. I said then
I wasn't going for no more draws. They don't know I
feel just like I did when my mama died. She got old
and gray and sat by the window till she died. She must
have done that 'cause she ain't had nothing else to do. I
was gone. My brother was gone. Sister gone. Everybody
gone. My daddy was gone. She sat there till she died. I
was staying down on Logan Street. Got the letter one
day and telegram the next. They usually fall on top of
one another ... but not that close. I got the letter say
"If you wanna see your mother you better come home."
Before I could get out the door the telegram came
saying, "It's too late ... your mother gone." I was trying
to borrow some money. Called the train station and
found out the schedule and I'm trying to borrow some

money. I can't go down there broke. I don't know how long I got to be there. I ain't even got the train fare. I got twelve dollars and sixty-three cents. I got the telegram and sat down and cried like a baby. I could beat any newborn baby in the world crying. I cried till the tears all run down in my ears. Got up and went out the door and everything looked different. Everything had changed. I felt like I had been cut loose. All them years something had a hold of me and I didn't know it. I didn't find out till it cut me loose. I walked out the door and everything had different colors to it. I felt great. I didn't owe nobody nothing. The last person I owed anything to was gone. I borrowed fifty dollars from West and went on down to her funeral. I come back and said, "Everybody better get out my way." You couldn't hold me down. It look like then I had somewhere to go fast. I didn't know where, but I damn sure was going there. That's the way I feel now. They don't know I got a clause of my own. I'll get up off the canvas if I have to. They can carry me out feet first ... but my clause say ... they got to meet my price!

Act 2, Scene 1

Holloway recounts the time he went to see Aunt Ester to take away his urge to kill his grandfather.

HOLLOWAY. Had two of them. One on my mother's side and one on my father's side. One of them I never knew. The other one wasn't no good for nobody. That was the worse Negro I ever known. He think if it wasn't for white people there wouldn't be no daylight. If you let him tell it, God was a white man who had a big plantation in the sky and sat around drinking mint juleps and smoking Havana cigars. He couldn't wait to die to get up in heaven to pick cotton. If he overheard you might wanna go down and get you some extra meat out the white man's smokehouse ... he'd run and tell him. He see you put a rabbit in your sack to weigh up with the cotton, he'd run and tell. The white man would give him a couple pounds of bacon. He'd bring that home and my grandmother would throw it out with the garbage. That's the kind of woman she was. I don't know how she got tied up with him. She used to curse the day she laid down with him. That rubbed off on me. I got a little older to where I could see what kind of man he was ... I figure if he want to go to heaven to pick cotton, I'd help him. I got real serious about it. It stayed on me so didn't nobody want to be around me 'cause of the bad energy I was carrying. Couldn't keep me a woman. Seemed like nothing wouldn't work out for me. I went up to see Aunt Ester and got that bad energy off me. And it worked too. Ask West. He died in his sleep. Caught pneumonia and laid down and died. They wouldn't let him in the hospital 'cause he didn't have any insurance. He crawled up in the bed in my grandmother's house and laid there till he died. March

5, 1952. So can't nobody tell me nothing about Aunt
Ester. I know what she can do for you.

Act 1, Scene 3

*Wolf describes his inability to become inti-
mate with any woman, citing the example of
Petey Brown killing his "old lady" at the Ellis
Hotel.*

WOLF. You right about that. It's hard to live in America.
Did you all hear when Petey Brown killed his old lady
last night? Caught her in the Ellis Hotel with his best
friend. Killed him too. That's why I don't have no one
woman. When I die every woman in Pittsburgh gonna
cry. They ain't gonna know what to do with themselves.
My woman come and told me she had another man. I
told her say, "All right, baby, but he can't hear and he
can't see. He can't see like I do. You got to be able to
pull a whole lot of boxcars to keep up with me." I'm like
Prophet Samuel ... if a man can get him seven women
... if he can find seven women or two more. Seven
women wanna lay down with him must see something
they like. Hell, it's hard to get one, let alone seven. It's
hard to get one you can trust that far. See, when you lay
down with her, you trusting her with your life. You lay
down you got to close your eyes. It wouldn't be nothing for somebody to walk up and slit your throat. That's
why you lock the door at night. You lock the door and it
be just you and her. That's a whole lot of trust there. If
I had that I wouldn't give it up for nothing. Other than
that when I die every woman in Pittsburgh gonna cry.

JITNEY

Act 1, Scene 1

Shealy believes his old girlfriend, Rosie, put a curse on him. Every time he lays down with another woman, he sees her face. He shares the story of the "yellow gal" who almost made him forget Rosie.

SHEALY. Naw she wasn't the one. I thought she was but then I believe Rosie done put a curse on me. She don't want me to have no other woman. But then she didn't want me. No, no, no. I told her baby, just tell me what kind of biscuits you want to make. I'm like the millman I can grind it up any way you want. She knew I was telling the truth to. She couldn't say nothing about that. She say you a poor man. What I need with a poor man? I told her say if I make a hundred I'll give you ninety-nine. She didn't trust me on that one but I went down to the crap game, I hit six quick licks, left with a hundred and sixty-three dollars. I went on back up there. She let me in. I lay a hundred dollars down on the table and told her, "Now, if I can just get one of them back I'd be satisfied." She reached down and handed me a dollar and I went on in the room and went to bed. I got up and she had my breakfast on the table. It wasn't soon long that ninety-nine dollars ran out and next thing I knew she had barred the door. I went on and left but I never could get her off my mind. I said I was gonna find me another woman. But every time I get hold to one ... time I lay down with them ... I see her face. I told myself the first time I lay down with a woman and don't see her face then that be the one I'm gonna marry. That be my little test. Now with that old yellow gal used to work down at Pope's I seen Rosie's face ... but it was blurry. Like a cloud of something come over it. I say, "I got to try this again. Maybe next time I won't see nothing." She told me she didn't want to see me no more. She told me come back same time tomorrow and if she changed her mind she'd leave the key in the mailbox. I went up there and there was one man in the house and two others sitting on the doorstep. I don't know who had the key.

Act 1, Scene 2

Rena comes to the station looking for her boyfriend, Youngblood. Turnbo, the neighborhood busybody, suggests she find an older, more responsible man and divulges that he has seen Youngblood driving around with her sister.

TURNBO. It ain't easy these days to raise a child. I don't know what's in these young boys' heads. Seem like they don't respect nobody. The don't even respect themselves. When I was coming along that was the first thing you learned. If you didn't respect yourself ... quite naturally you couldn't respect nobody else. When I was coming along the more respect you had for other people ... the more people respected you. Seem like it come back to you double. These young boys don't know nothing about that ... and it's gonna take them a lifetime to find out. They disrespect everybody and don't think nothing about it. They steal their own grandmother's television. Get hold of one woman ... time another one walk by they grab hold to her. Don't even care who it is. It could be anybody. I just try to live and let live. My grandmother was like that. She the one raised me. She didn't care what nobody else done as long as it didn't cross her path. She was a good woman. She taught me most everything I know. She wouldn't let you lie. That was just about the worst thing you could be. A liar didn't know the truth and was never gonna find out. And everybody know it's the truth what set you free. Now I ain't trying to get in your business or nothing. Like I say I just live and let live. But some things just come up on you wrong and you have to say something about it otherwise it throw your whole life off balance. I know you don't want to hear this ... but you don't need no hotheaded young boy like Youngblood. What you need is somebody level-headed who know how to respect and appreciate a woman ... I can see the kind of woman you is. You ain't the kind of woman for Youngblood and he ain't the kind of man for you. You need a more mature ... responsible man.

Act 1, Scene 2

*Rena is trying her best to keep her family
together, while going to school, working and
raising a child. When the food money goes
missing, she angrily confronts Youngblood.*

RENA. Darnell I don't understand. I try so hard. I'm doing
everything I can to try and make this work. I'm working my little job down there at the restaurant ... going
to school ... trying to take care of Jesse ... trying to take
care of your needs ... trying to keep the house together
... trying to make everything better. Now, I come home
from work I got to go to the store. I go upstairs and
look in the drawer and the food money is gone. Now
you explain that to me. There was eighty dollars in the
drawer that ain't in there now.

What you need it for? You tell me. What's more important than me and Jesse eating?

You know I don't touch the grocery money. Whatever
happens, we got to eat. If I need clothes ... I do without. My little personal stuff ... I do without. If I ain't
got no electricity ... I do without ... but I don't never
touch the grocery money. 'Cause I'm not gonna be that
irresponsible to my child. 'Cause he depend on me. I'm
not going to be that irresponsible to my family. I ain't
gonna be like that. Jesse gonna have a chance at life. He
ain't going to school hungry 'cause I spent the grocery
money on some nail polish or some Afro Sheen. He
ain't gonna be laying up in the bed hungry and unable
to sleep 'cause his daddy took the grocery money to pay
a debt.

You know what you be doing better than I but whatever it is it ain't enough. It ain't all about the money,
Darnell. I'm talking about the way you been doing. You

ain't never home no more. You be out half the night. I
wake up and you ain't there.

Act 1, Scene 4

Booster has just been released from a twenty-year prison sentence. He comes to visit his father, Becker, at the jitney station. In this emotional reunion, he tells his father about the first time he realized Becker wasn't as big and strong, nor as admirable, as he thought when he was a little boy.

Optional cut for time purposes: End with "That's when I told myself if I ever got big I wouldn't let nothing make me small."

BOOSTER. Yeah Pop, you taught me a lot of things. And a lot of things I had to learn on my own. Like that time Mr. Rand came to the house to collect the rent when we was two months behind. I don't remember what year it was. I just know it was winter. Grandma Ada had just died and you got behind in the rent 'cause you had to help pay for her funeral.

I don't know if you knew it Pop, but you were a big man. Everywhere you went people treated you like a big man. You used to take me to the barbershop with you. You'd walk in there and fill up the whole place. Everybody would stop cussing because Jim Becker had walked in. I would just look at you and wonder how you could be that big. I wanted to be like that. I would go to school and try to make myself feel big. But I never could. I told myself that's okay ... when I get grown I'm gonna be big like that. Walk into the barbershop and have everybody stop and look at me.

That day when Mr. Rand come to the house it was snowing. You came out on the porch and he started shouting and cussing and threatening to put us out in the street where we belonged.

I was waiting for you to tell him to shut up ... to get off your porch. But you just looked at him and promised you would have the money next month. Mama came to the door and Mr. Rand kept shouting and cussing. I looked at Mama ... she was trying to get me to go in the house ... and I looked at you ... and you had got smaller. The longer he shouted the smaller you got. When we went back to the barbershop you didn't seem so big no more. You was the same size as everybody else. You was just another man in the barbershop. That's when I told myself if I ever got big I wouldn't let nothing make me small.

Then when I met Susan McKnight and found out her daddy was the Vice President of Gulf Oil ... that's when I got big. That made me a big man. I felt like I was somebody. I felt like I could walk in the barbershop and fill it up the way you did. Then when she told that lie on me that's when I woke up. That's when I realized that I wasn't big from the inside. I wasn't big on my own. When she told that lie it made me small. I wanted to do something that said I wasn't just another nigger ... that I was Clarence Becker. I wanted to make them remember my name. And I thought about you standing there and getting small and Mr. Rand shouting and Susan McKnight shouting out that lie and I realized it was my chance to make the Beckers big again ... my chance to show what I had learned on my own. I thought you would understand. I thought you would be proud of me.

Act 1, Scene 4

After Booster insults Becker's life choices,
Becker tells Booster why he never came to see
him during his twenty-year prison sentence.

BECKER. I kept seeing your face at your mother's funeral.
How you just stood there and never shed a tear. Stood
there with a scowl on your face. And now you want to
come in here and ridicule me 'cause I didn't knock Mr.
Rand on his ass. You wanna know why? I'll tell you why.
Because I had your black ass crying to be fed. Crying
to have a roof over your head. To have clothes to wear
to school and lunch money in your pocket. That's why!
Because I had a family. I had responsibility. If I had
knocked him on his ass you would have went hungry.
You wouldn't have had clothes on your back or a roof
over your head. I done what I had to do. I swallowed
my pride and let them mess over me, all the time saying
"You bastards got it coming. Look out! Becker's Boy's
coming to straighten this shit out! You're not gonna
fuck over him! He's gonna grow big and strong! Watch
out for Becker's Boy! Becker's taking this ass whipping
so his boy can stride through this shit like Daniel in the
lion's den! Watch out for Becker's Boy!" *(He has worked
himself into a frenzy and is now near tears.)* And what
I get, huh? You tell me. What I get? Tell me what I get!
Tell me! What I get? What I get, huh? Stay away from
me! What I get, huh? What I get? Tell me?

    (Booster is silent.)

I get a murderer, that's what. A murderer.

And the way your mama loved you. You killed her! You
know that? You a double murderer! That woman took
sick the day that judge sentenced you and she ain't
never walked or said another word or ate another thing
for twenty-three days. She just laid up in that room

until she died. Now you tell me that ain't killing her.
Tell me that ain't killing her!

Act 1, Scene 4

Booster accuses Becker of not caring for his mother properly while he was on trial. Becker claims he did all that was humanly possible for his wife, insisting that it was her son's death sentence that made her die of grief. Becker renounces any further contact with his son.

BECKER. I was there! I was holding her had when she died. Where was you? Locked up in a cage like some animal. That's what killed her. To hear the judge say that the life she brought in the world was unfit to live. That you be "remanded to the custody of the Commissioner of Corrections at Western State Penitentiary and there to be executed in the electric chair. This order to be carried out thirty days from today." Ain't that what the judge said? Ain't that what she heard? "This order to be carried out thirty days from today." That's what killed her. She didn't want to live them thirty days. She didn't want to be alive to hear on the eleven o'clock news that they had killed you. So don't you say nothing to me about turning my back when I nursed that woman, talked to her, held her hand, prayed over her and the last words to come out of her mouth was your name. I was there! Where were you Mr. Murderer. Mr. Unfit to Live Amongst Society. Where were you when your mama was dying and calling your name. You are my son. I helped bring you into this world. But from this moment on ... I'm calling the deal off. You ain't nothing to me, boy. You just another nigger on the street.

Act 2, Scene 1

Doub, a Korean War vet, speaks to
Youngblood, a Vietnam War vet, about his
experience in the army. He points out that
things are different now for Youngblood. He
advises him to go to school and do something
more fulfilling with his future than just driv-
ing jitneys.

DOUB. You ain't the only one they sent. They sent a whole
lot of other folks too. Some of them wasn't lucky
enough to make it back alive. You ain't the only one
been in the army. I went into the army in '50. Looking
to make something of myself. That was after the war.
I didn't know they was gonna pull out a map stick a
pin in it and say, "Let's go kill some people over here."
I wasn't in the Army but four months and they had me
in Korea. Second Division. Company B. 4th Battalion.
It was a detail company. I think at the time the only
dead body I had seen was my grandmama when Foster
buried her. That's all I knew about a dead body. But I
was meant to find out quick. The third day they put us
on some trucks and drove out to the front lines. I was
scared as I could get. The last words I remember my
mama saying to me was how she was praying I didn't
get sent to the front lines. I wasn't in Korea but three
days and here I was on the front lines. Got out there
and everything was quiet. The sergeant told us to get
down off the trucks. We got down and started walking. Got near about two hundred yards when we saw
our first body. Then another one. Then three more. The
sergeants say "alright boys, we gonna clean up. I want
you to stack the bodies six high." I never will forget
that. "I want you to stack the bodies six high." Not five.
Not seven. Six high. And that's what I did for the next
nine months. Clean up the battlefield. It took me six

months before I got to where I could keep my supper down. After that it didn't bother me no more. Never did learn how to do nothing else. They was supposed to teach me but they never did. They just never paid me no mind. There was a whole bunch of us they never paid no mind. What I'm trying to tell you is the white man ain't got no personal war against you 'cause you buying a house and they gonna tear down this block. You too young to be depending on driving jitneys. Is that what you want to do all your life?

How old are you? Twenty-four? Why don't you go to school under the GI bill? Become something. Make something of your life. You can be anything you want. Be a pilot or a engineer or something. Like I tell my boys, the world's opened up to you. When I was your age, the only thing you could get a job doing was bussing dishes, running elevators and cleaning out toilets. Things like that. It ain't like that now. You can be anything you want. You're young, act kinda crazy, but you got some sense. You don't waste your money. You got sense enough to buy a house. Go on to school, Youngblood. You too young to be counting on driving jitneys.

Act 2, Scene 1

When Youngblood finally reveals the reason he's been with Rena's sister and why he's been working all hours of the night and day, he proudly tells Rena that he has bought a house for their family. She, in turn, has a reaction he was not expecting. She is angry that she wasn't included in this very important decision.

RENA. Darnell, you ain't bought no house without me. How many times in your life do you get to pick out a house?

You can't just surprise me with a house and I'm supposed to say, "Oh, Darnell, that's nice." At one time I would have. But I'm not seventeen no more. I have responsibilities. I want to know if it has a hookup for a washer and dryer 'cause I got to wash Jesse's clothes. I want to know if it has a yard and do it have a fence and how far Jesse has to go to school. I ain't thinking about where to put the TV. That's not what's important to me. And you supposed to know, Darnell. You supposed to know what's important to me like I'm supposed to know what's important to you. I'm not asking you to do it by yourself. I'm here with you. We in this together. See ... house or no house we still ain't got the food money. But if you had come and told me ... if you had shared that with me ... we could have went to my mother and we could have got eighty dollars for the house and still had money for food. You just did it all wrong Darnell. I mean, you did the right thing but you did it wrong.

Act 2, Scene 1

Youngblood feels hurt by Rena's reaction but quickly points out that he is a changed man and that he wants to become a better man for their son and her.

YOUNGBLOOD. No matter what I do it's gonna come out wrong with you. That's why you jump to conclusions. That's why you accused me of running around with Peaches. You can't look and see that I quit going to parties all the time ... that I quit running with Barbra and Earl ... that I quit chasing women. You just look at me and see the old Darnell. If you can't change the way you look at me ... then I may as well surrender now. I can't beat your memory of who I was if you can't see I've changed. I go out here and work like a dog to try and do something nice for you and no matter what I do, I can't never do it right 'cause all you see is the way I used to be. You don't see the new Darnell. You don't see I've changed.

No, Rena ... people believe what they want to believe ... what they set up in their mind to believe. I know what it looked like when I was gone all the time and not bringing home any money. But you could have noticed that I was tired ... you could have said "Darnell ain't talking too much 'cause he's tired." You could have noticed that I didn't act like somebody running the streets ... that I didn't come home smelling like alcohol and perfume ... that I didn't dress like somebody running the streets. If you had thought it all the way through, you could have noticed how excited I was when I got the UPS job ... how I asked you if I could take it ... you would have noticed how I was planning things ... that I wasn't sitting around drinking beer and playing cards ... how I would get up early on Sunday and go out to the airport to try to make a few extra dollars before the jitney station opened. But you ain't seen all that. You ain't seen the new Darnell. You still working off your memory. But the past is over and done with. I'm thinking about the future. You not the only one who thinks about Jesse. That's why I'm trying to do something different. That's why I'm trying to buy a house. Maybe I should have told you about the house. Maybe I did do it wrong. But I done it. I tried to show you I loved you but what did I get for it?

KING HEDLEY II

Act 1, Scene 2

Elmore describes the dangers he faced in the old days when he was a gambler, a thief, and when he met Ruby. In this story, he gives an account of an entire day and calls himself "lucky" at the end of it, because he comes out even.

ELMORE. Money ain't nothing. I ain't had but a dollar sixty-seven cents when I met your mama. I had a hundred-dollar Stetson hat, a pint of gin and a razor. That and a dollar sixty-seven cents. I'm walking around with a hundred-dollar hat and a dollar and sixty-seven cents in my pocket. I told myself, "Something wrong. This ain't working out right." The razor was my daddy's razor. He had cut him eleven niggers with that razor. Had good weight to it. Felt nice in your hands. Make you wanna cut somebody. The pint of gin I had just borrowed from the after-hour joint. I stepped outside and saw her standing there. I asked her name and she told me. Told me say, "My name's Ruby." And somehow that fit her like she was a jewel or something precious. That's what I told her say, "You must be precious to somebody." She told me she ain't had nobody. We got to talking and one thing led to another. I took and spent a dollar sixty cents on her. Bought me a nickel cigar. Now I got a razor, a pint of gin, a hundred-dollar Stetson, a cigar, two cents and a woman. I was ready for whatever was out there. I woke up in the morning and felt lucky. Pawned my Stetson. Got seven dollars and went down the gambling joint. Playing dollar tonk. Left out of there broke. She back at my place waiting on me. I got to at least bring dinner. I looked up and seen a white fellow standing on the corner. He wasn't doing anything. Just standing there. Had on a gray hat. I told myself, "He got some money." I walked right on by. I didn't look at him. When I got even with him, I threw him up against the wall. I told myself I wasn't gonna use my razor unless I had to. He gave me his money and I started to run. I can't walk away. I'm running but I ain't running fast. I heard the bullet when it passed me. That's a sound I don't never want to hear again. You can hear the air move. When that bullet split the air, it make a sound. If you don't know I will tell you. You can fly. I was running so fast my feet wasn't touching the ground. Yet I moving through the air. What I'm doing? I'm flying. Ain't nothing else you can call it. I got away and told myself I was lucky. Then I knew why I had woke up feeling like that. When I got to where I could look in my hand to see what I had. I looked down and I had seven dollars. I told myself, hell, if I could get fifty cents I can go back and get my hat out of the pawn shop. Call it even. Start over again tomorrow.

Act 1, Scene 2

Tonya and King are fighting over Tonya's decision to have an abortion. She believes that she's too old to have another child; her own teenage daughter has a baby. Tonya doesn't want to add one more life to this turbulent world only to have him/her become yet another victim.

TONYA. Why? Look at Natasha. I couldn't give her what she needed. Why I wanna go back and do it again? I ain't got nothing else to give. I can't give myself. How I'm gonna give her? I don't understand what to do ... how to be a mother. You either love too much or don't love enough. Don't seem like there's no middle ground. I look up, she ten years old and I'm still trying to figure out life. Figure out what happened. Next thing I know she grown. Talking about she a woman. Just 'cause you can lay down and open your legs to a man don't make you a woman. I tried to tell her that. She's a baby! She don't know nothing about life. What she know? Who taught her? I'm trying to figure it out myself. Time I catch up, it's moved on to something else. I got to watch her being thrown down a hole it's gonna take her a lifetime to crawl out and I can't do nothing to help her. I got to stand by and watch her. Why I wanna go back through all that? I don't want to have a baby that younger than my grandchild. Who turned the world around like that? What sense that make? I'm thirty-five years old. Don't seem like there's nothing left. I'm through with babies. I ain't raising no more. Ain't raising no grandkids. I'm looking out for Tonya. I ain't raising no kid to have somebody shoot him. To have his friends shoot him. To have the police shoot him. Why I want to bring another life into this world that don't respect life? I don't want to raise no more babies when you got to fight to keep them alive.

Act 1, Scene 2

*Tonya continues to fight for her decision to
end her pregnancy by painting a picture of a
desolate mother who lost her son to violence.
She firmly states that she is not having this
child.*

TONYA. You take Little Buddy Will's mother up on Bryn
Mawr Road. What she got? A heartache that don't
never go away. She up there now sitting down in her
living room. She got to sit down 'cause she can't stand
up. She sitting down trying to figure it out. Trying to
figure out what happened. One minute her house is full
of life. The next minute it's full of death. She was wait
ing for him to come home and they bring her a corpse.
Say, "Come down and make the identification. Is this
your son?" Got a tag on his toe say "John Doe". They got
to put a number on it. John Doe number four. She got
the dinner on the table. Say, "Junior like fried chicken."
She got some of that. Say, "Junior like string beans." She
got some of that. She don't know Junior ain't eating no
more. He got a pile of clothes she washing up. She don't
know Junior don't need no more clothes. She look in
the closet. Junior ain't got no suit. She got to go buy
him a suit. He can't try it on. She got to guess the size.
Somebody come up and tell her, "Miss So-and-So, your
boy got shot." She know before they say it. Her knees
start to get weak. She shaking her head. She don't
want to hear it. Somebody call the police. They come
and pick him up off the sidewalk. Dead nigger on Bryn
Mawr Road. They got to quit playing cards and come
and pick him up. They used to take pictures.

They don't even take pictures no more. They pull him
out of the freezer and she look at him. She don't want
to look. They make her look. What to do now? The only
thing to do is call the undertaker. The line is busy.

She got to call back five times. The undertaker got so much business he don't know what to do. He losing sleep. He got to hire two more helpers to go with the two he already got. He don't even look at the bodies no more. He couldn't tell you what they look like. He only remember the problems he have with them. This one so big and fat if he fall off the table it take six men to pick him up. That one ain't got no cheek. That one eyes won't stay closed. The other one been dead so long he got maggots coming out his nose. The family can't pay for that one. The coroner wants to see the other one again. That one's mother won't go home. The other one ... I ain't going through that. I ain't having this baby ... and I ain't got to explain it to nobody.

Act 1, Scene 2

*After Tonya shares her frustration with
Ruby, the older woman recounts her past
when she was pregnant with King. Back then
she sought Aunt Ester's help in seeking an
abortion. Quite surprisingly, the spiritual
healer told her how special her son would be
and gave her sound advice about the rhythm
of life.*

RUBY. I done tried everything I know. King don't believe I
love him. It's a mother's love. It don't never go away. I
love me but I love King more. Sometimes I might not
love me but there don't never come a time I don't love
him. He don't understand that.

King don't know he lucky to be here. I didn't want to
have no baby. Seem to me like I got off to a bad start.
I wanted to have an abortion. Somebody sent me up
there to see Aunt Ester. I thought she did abortions.
It didn't take me long to find out I was in the wrong
place. She was sitting in a room with a red curtain. A
little old woman wearing a stocking cap. I can't say if
she had any teeth or not. She was just sitting there.
Told me to come closer where she could put her hands
on my head. I got real peaceful. Seem like all my problems went away. She told me man can plant the seed
but only God can make it grow. Told me God was a
good judge. I told her that's what scared me. She just
laughed and told me, "God has three hands. Two for
that baby and one for the rest of us." That's just the way
she said it. "God got three hands. Two for that baby
and one for the rest of us. You got your time coming."
I never will forget that. I used to look at King and try
and figure it out. But I ain't seen nothing to make her
say that. I thought maybe she was just telling me that
but she ain't supposed to lie about nothing like that. I

just ain't never seen nothing that would make him that special. That's what I'm telling you about that baby you carrying. You never know what God have planned. You can't all the time see it. That's what Louise used to tell me. You can't all the time see it but God can see it good.

Life's got its own rhythm. It don't always go along with your rhythm. It don't always be what you think it's gonna be. *(Starts to exit into the house.)*

That's all life is ... trying to match up them two rhythms. You ever match them up and you won't have to worry about nothing.

Act 1, Scene 3

Angry over having his receipt not count when he attempted to pick up his photos at Sears, King describes his life-long struggle for meaning, purpose, and respect.

KING. My fifth-grade teacher told me I was gonna make a good janitor. Say she can tell that by how good I erased the blackboards. Had me believing it. I come home and told Mama Louise I wanted to be a janitor. She told me I could be anything I wanted. I say, "Okay I'll be a janitor." I thought that was what I was supposed to be. I didn't know no better. That was the first job I got. Cleaning up that bar used to be down on Wylie. Got one job the man told me he was gonna shoot me if he caught me stealing anything. I ain't worked for him ten minutes. I quit right there. He calling me a thief before I start. Neesi told me I shouldn't have quit. But I'm a man. I don't bother nobody. And I know right from wrong. I know what's right for me. That's where me and the rest of the people part ways. Tonya ask me say, "When we gonna move?" She want a decent house. One the plaster ain't falling off the walls. I say, "Okay but I got to wait." What I'm waiting on? I don't know. I'm just waiting. I told myself I'm waiting for things to change. That mean I'm gonna be living here forever. Tonya deserve better than that. I go for a job and they say, "What can you do." I say, "I can do anything. If you give me the tanks and the airplanes I can go out there and win any war that's out there."

I can dance all night if the music's right. Ain't nothing I can't do. I could build a railroad if I had the steel and a gang of men to drive the spikes. I ain't limited to nothing. I can go down there and do Mellon's job. I know how to count money. I don't loan money to everybody who ask me. I know how to do business. I'm talking about mayor ... governor, I can do it all. I ain't got no limits. I know right from wrong. I know which way the wind blow too. It don't blow my way. Mellon got six houses. I ain't got none. But that don't mean he six times a better man than me.

Act 1, Scene 3

King speaks to Elmore and Mister about the many injustices he's faced, the most egregious being when he was found guilty of killing the man that cut his face brutally.

KING. I ain't sorry for nothing I done. And ain't gonna be sorry. I'm gonna see to that. 'Cause I'm gonna do the right thing. Always. It ain't in me to do nothing else. We might disagree about what that is. But I know what is right for me. As long as I draw a breath in my body I'm gonna do the right thing for me. What I got to be sorry for? People say, "Ain't you sorry you killed Pernell?" I ain't sorry I killed Pernell. The nigger deserve to die. He cut my face. I told the judge, "Not Guilty." They thought I was joking. I say, "The motherfucker cut me! How can I be wrong for killing him?" That's common sense. I don't care what the law say. The law don't understand this. It must not. They wanna take and lock me up. Where's the understanding? If a burglar break in a white man's house to steal his TV and the white man shoot him they don't say he wrong. The law understand that. They pat him on the back and tell him to go on home.

You see what I'm saying? The jury come back and say, "Guilty." They asked them one by one. They all said, "Guilty." Had nine white men and three white women. They all said, "Guilty." They wouldn't look at me. I told them to look at me. Look at that scar.

I got closer to where they could see my scar. The judge like to had a fit. They had six deputies come at me from all sides. They said I tried to attack the jury. I was just trying to get closer so they could see my face. They tried to run out the door. They took and put me in solitary confinement. Said I was unruly.

Act 2, Scene 2

King continues to justify his actions by describing in detail the day he killed Pernell.

KING. I don't know about you and Leroy but Pernell made me kill him. Pernell called me "champ". I told him my name's King. He say, "Yeah, champ." I go on. I don't say nothing. I told myself, "He don't know." He don't know my daddy killed a man for calling him out of his name. He don't know he fucking with King Hedley II. I got the atomic bomb as far as he's concerned. And I got to use it. They say God looks after fools and drunks. I used to think that was true. But seeing as how he was both ... I don't know anymore. He called me "champ" and I didn't say nothing. I put him on probation. Told myself he don't know but I'm gonna give him a chance to find out. If he find out and come and tell me he's sorry then I'll let him live. I'm gonna fuck him up. I'm gonna bust both his kneecaps. But I'm gonna let him live. Saturday. I don't know why it's always on a Saturday. Saturday I went up to buy me some potatoes. I say, "I want to have some mashed potatoes." I told Neesi say, "You get the milk and butter and I'll get the potatoes." I went right up there to Hester's on Wylie. I went up there and got me ten pound of potatoes. I started to get twenty but they only had one bag and it was tore, the bag was tore. I didn't want them to spill out on the way home. If I had been carrying twenty pounds of potatoes maybe I would have went home a shorter way. I say, "Let me breeze by Centre Avenue on my way home and let me see if I see Charlie. He owe me twenty dollars and if he pay me that might bring me some luck." I got halfway down there and I seen Pernell. First thing I tell myself is, "I ain't gonna be nobody's champ today." I fix that hard in my head and I try to walk past him. I didn't want to ignore him so I

say, "How you doing, Pernell?" I don't really care how
he doing. I'm just being polite like Mama Louise taught
me. No sooner than the words got out my mouth then
I felt something hot on my face. A hot flash and then
something warm and wet. This nigger done cut me! He
hit me with that razor and I froze. I didn't know what
happened. It was like somebody turned on a light and
it seem like everything stood still and I could see him
smiling. Then he ran. I didn't know which way he ran.
I was still blinded by that light. It took the doctor four
hours and a hundred and twelve stitches to sew me up.
I say, "That's all right, the King is still here." But I figure
that scar got to mean something. I can't take it off. It's
part of me now. I figure it's got to mean something. As
long as Pernell was still walking around it wasn't nothing but a scar. I had to give it some meaning.

It wasn't but two weeks later and I'm thinking about
this thing. I'm thinking what it gonna mean to everybody. I thought about his mama. I thought the whole
thing out. It ain't easy to take somebody's life. I told
myself, "It's me or him," even though I knew that was
a lie. I saw his funeral. I heard the preacher. I saw the
undertaker. I saw the gravediggers. I saw the flowers.
And then I see his woman. That's the hardest part. She
know him better than anybody. She know what makes
him bleed. She know why he breathes, what he sound
like when he wakes up in the morning. She know when
he's hungry and what will satisfy him. She know everything what nobody else don't know. It was hard but I
told myself she got to suffer. She got to play the widow.
She got to cry the tears.

About two weeks later I saw Pernell going into Irv's
bar. He went straight back to the phone booth. I don't
know who he was calling but that was the last call he
made. I saw my scar in the window of the phone booth.
I tapped on the glass. He turned and looked and froze

right there. The first bullet hit him in the mouth. I don't
know where the other fourteen went. The only regret is
I didn't get away. I didn't get away with murder that
time. You always regret the one you don't get away
with. Cost me seven years of my life. But I done got
smarter. The next one's gonna be self-defense. The next
one ain't gonna cost me nothing.

Act 2, Scene 3

Ruby shares with Tonya moments from her past when she was a singer in Walter Kelly's band. He once assaulted her in a car, but she valiantly fought back.

RUBY. Walter Kelly was a big man with jet black hair. Brown-skinned man played a trumpet and I sang in his band for a while. He tried to make love to me but I didn't want no part of him 'cause he was too good-looking and he already had a gang of women. Everybody expected 'cause I sang in his band that he could do with me like he wanted. He thought that at one time himself but I got him straight on that. We was sitting in his car. He had a car with a top you could put down. We was having a drink and just laughing and singing and fooling around when he put his hand under my dress. I had men put their hand under my dress before. They want to see what you got. They like to see how it fit in their hand. They say they can tell what kind of woman you is. Walter Kelly got his hand all the way up under my dress and he touched me there. I told him to stop. He just laughed. We was drinking from a pint bottle. I took the bottle and broke it on the car handle. I cut my hand pretty bad but I put the glass up to his throat. Blood was running all down my hand and everywhere. I told him to lick it. I told him I wanted him to taste my blood 'cause if he didn't move his hand from under my dress I was gonna taste his. I rubbed my hand all over his face. There was blood everywhere. My hand looked like it wasn't gonna stop bleeding. He moved his hand and I got out of the car. I found out later I was on my period and I got mad. I told myself I wished I had cut him 'cause there wasn't nobody's blood in the car but mine.

Act 2, Scene 3

King uses his growing plants that are sur-
viving the rocky soil they were planted in
as a metaphor for Tonya to have faith in
her baby's future. Despite the violence on the
street, this child might flourish.

KING. Tonya. Look at that. That dirt's hard. That dirt's
rocky. But it still growing. It's gonna open up and it's
gonna be beautiful. I ain't never looked at no flower
before. I ain't never tried to grow none. I was coming
out the drug store and they had them seeds on the
counter. I say, "I'm gonna try this. Grow Tonya some
flowers. I ain't got nothing to lose but a dollar. I'll pay a
dollar to see how it turn out." Ruby told me they wasn't
gonna grow. Made me feel like I should have left them
there at the drugstore. But then they grew. Elmore
stepped on them and they still growing. That's what
made me think of Pernell. Pernell stepped on me and
I pulled his life out by the root. What does that make
me? It don't make me a big man. Most people see me
coming and they go the other way. They wave from
across the street. People look at their hands funny after
they shake my hand. They try to pretend they don't see
my scar when that's all they looking at. I used to think
Pernell did that to me. But I did it to myself. Pernell
put that scar on my face, but I put the bigger mark on
myself. That's why I need this baby, not 'cause I took
something out the world but because I wanna put
something in it. Let everybody know I was here. You
got King Hedley II and then you got King Hedley III.
Got rocky dirt. Got glass and bottles. But it still deserve
to live. Even if you do have to call the undertaker. Even
if somebody come along and pull it out by the root. It
still deserve to live. It still deserve that chance. I'm here
and I ain't going nowhere. I need to have that baby. Do
you understand?

Act 2, Scene 3

Tonya finally agrees to have the baby but gives King a stern condition. She doesn't want him to steal money to buy her things. She simply wants him to be present for the baby and for her.

TONYA. King, you don't understand. I don't want everything. That's not why I'm living ... to want things. I done lived thirty-five years without things. I got enough for me. I just want to wake up in the bed beside you in the morning. I don't need things. I saw what they cost. I can live without them and be happy. I ain't asking you to stop living. The things I want you can't buy with money. And it seem like they be the hardest to get. Why? When they be the simplest. Do your job but understand what it is. It ain't for you to go out of here and steal money to get me things. Your job is to be around so this baby can know you its daddy. Do that. For once, somebody do that. Be that. That's how you be a man, anything else I don't want.

Act 2, Scene 4

After Elmore gives an account of when he killed Ruby's boyfriend, Leroy, Ruby shares her side of the story.

RUBY. They showed me the body. They come up and got me. His sister had gone to Mobile and they asked me to come down and see if it was him. I didn't want to look. I grabbed hold my arm and just squeezed. He had his mouth open. That's what I always will remember. Wasn't much more there. He was shot five times in the head. I looked away and something told me to look back. One shot had hit him in the nose and it just wasn't there no more. I don't know where it was. It wasn't on his face. They asked me did I know him. I told them, naw, I didn't know him, I ain't had a chance to find out too much about him. I told them I knew who it was. "That's Leroy Slater. I was living with him at 131 Warren Street." They asked me to sign some papers. One man told me he was sorry. I left out of there and walked on back home. That was the saddest day.

I couldn't look at Elmore after I found out what he had done. Even though I loved him, it was a long time before I could look at him. I felt so sad. I said I was gonna quit living. I stole away and cried. I didn't want nobody to see me. I felt like I was about to lose my mind. I cried and then I dried my eyes. Then I'd cry again. Seem like the world had gone crazy. Then everything stopped. They carried him on out there and put him in the ground. Leroy Slater. A good man. I never will forget him. They say life have its own rhythm. I wish it didn't have none like that. That was the saddest I ever been.

RADIO GOLF

Act 1, Scene 1

Roosevelt is running a golf camp for Pittsburgh kids. He tells Harmond about the power he felt the first time he hit a golf ball and how he wants to pass that empowerment on to a new generation of black Americans.

ROOSEVELT. I signed up two more kids last week. That makes eighteen. I just want these kids to know what it feels like to hit a golf ball. I hit my first golf ball I asked myself where have I been? How'd I miss this? I couldn't believe it. I felt free. Truly free. For the first time. I watched the ball soar down the driving range. I didn't think it could go so high. It just kept going higher and higher. I felt something lift off of me. Some weight I was carrying around and didn't know it. I felt like the world was open to me. Everything and everybody. I never did feel exactly like that anymore. I must have hit a hundred golf balls trying to get that feeling. But that first time was worth everything. I felt like I had my dick in my hand and was waving it around like a club. "I'm a man! Anybody want some of this come and get it!" That was the best feeling of my life.

That's why I keep my golf clubs in the trunk of my car just in case I drive by a golf course. I keep looking for that feeling. That's what I want these kids to have. That'll give them a chance at life. I wish somebody had come along and taught me how to play golf when I was ten. That'll set you on a path to life where everything is open to you. You don't have to hide and crawl under a rock just 'cause you black. Feel like you don't belong in the world.

Act 1, Scene 4

*Sterling tries to convince Harmond to give
him a job with a redevelopment project in the
Hill District. Sterling, however, won't easily
fit the profile of an average construction
worker. Being a black man, he has always
had to do things his own way.*

STERLING. Naw ... you don't understand. I'm my own union.
I got my own everything. Except my own bank. But I
got my own truck. I got my own tools. I got my own
rules and I got my own union. I don't play no games.
I have to have my own. That's the only way I got anything. I've been going through the back door all my
life. See, people get confused about me. They did that
ever since we was in school. But I know how to row the
boat. I been on the water a long time. I know what it
takes to plug the holes. I ain't dumb. Even though some
people think I am. That give me an advantage. I found
that out when I was in the orphanage. Mr. Redwood
taught me that. He told me, "You ain't dumb, you just
faster than everybody else." I was so fast it made me
look slow. I was waiting for them to catch up ... that
made it look like I was standing around doing nothing. They kept me behind in the fourth grade 'cause I
wouldn't add twelve and twelve. I thought it was stupid.
Everybody know there's twelve to a dozen and twenty-
four to two dozen. I don't care if it's donuts or oranges.
They handed me the test and I turned it in blank. If
you had seventeen dollars and you bought a parrot for
twelve dollars how many dollars would you have left?
Who the hell gonna spend twelve dollars on a parrot?
What you gonna do with it? Do you know how many
chickens you can buy for twelve dollars? They thought
I didn't know the answer. Every time somebody come
to adopt me they say, "Well, Sterling's a little slow." That

stuck with me. I started to believe it myself. Maybe they knew something I didn't know. That's when Mr. Redwood told me, "You ain't dumb. You just faster than everybody else." I've been going in the back doors all my life 'cause they don't never let me in the front.

Act 1, Scene 4

After seeing Harmond's flag pin, Old Joe tells Sterling and Harmond the significance of the American flag in his long life.

OLD JOE. Lots of men died under that flag. That American flag was everywhere. Joe Mott carried it into battle but it was everywhere. In the mess hall. In the dance hall. We had a great big mess hall and they would bring the women in from the town and we'd have a great big old dance. You look up and there would be that flag hanging behind the bandstand. That flag was everywhere. You saw it in the morning when you woke up and you saw it at night before you went to bed. Sometimes you saw it in your sleep. When the time come and I saw Joe Mott fall with that flag ... shot right through the head ... bullet went in one end and come out the other ... I don't know where it went after that. When I saw him fall I said, "No, I ain't gonna let you get away with nothing like that." That's what I said when I picked up that flag. This the flag on this side of the battle. That's what side I'm on. Joe Mott ain't died for nothing. If his life don't mean nothing then my life don't mean nothing. I had sense enough to see that. A lot of people can't see that. I can't let him die and let the flag lay there. I was the closest one to it. I didn't even think about it. I just picked it up. I picked it up and carried it right up to the day I got discharged. December 4, 1945. I got out the Army and went and saw Joe Mott's mother. She live down in Georgia. I went down there and saw her. Walking down the street a white fellow stopped me. Reached up and tore my flag off my coat. Told me I ain't had no right to walk around with an American flag. I hope they let you keep yours.

Act 2, Scene 4

*Mame is marking a crossroad in her relation-
ship with Harmond. She still loves him but
she is disturbed to see him making choices she
cannot condone.*

MAME. I got a call this morning from the governor's office.
They cancelled my next interview and said they didn't
want to reschedule any further interviews with me at
this time.

You jumped but I'm falling too. I'm the wife of
Harmond Wilks. That's all the governor sees. All any of
the other board members see. What all our friends see.
I tied myself so tight to you that there is no me. I don't
know if I can carry this any further.

I have a center too. What happens when that caves
in? I have questions too. You're acting like a kid who,
because things don't go his way, takes his ball and goes
home. That's what your problem is. You've always been
the kid who had the ball. You're the one with the glove
and the bat. You had the bike when nobody else had
one. All your life you always had everything go your
way.

I'm still standing here Harmond. I still love you. But
this is all you now. Your campaign, that old house, the
Hill ... You're on your own with all that. I can't live my
life for you. And you can't live yours for me. But I'm
still standing here.

See you tonight.

Act 2, Scene 4

Harmond and Roosevelt see the value of Aunt Ester's house completely differently. Roosevelt sees it as just a question of money, therefore common sense. Harmond disagrees. Moreover, it has now become painfully apparent that the rules he has been trying to follow change according to who's in power.

HARMOND WILKS. No. Common sense says that ain't right. We see it different. No matter what you always on the edge. If you go to the center you look up and find everything done shifted and the center is now the edge. The rules change every day. You got to change with them. After awhile the edge starts to get worn. You don't notice it at first but you're fraying with it. Oh, no, look ... We got a black mayor. We got a black CEO. The head of our department is black. We couldn't possibly be prejudiced. Got two hundred and fourteen people work in the department and two blacks but we couldn't possibly be race-conscious. Look, we even got a black football coach. You guys can sing. You can run fast. Boy, I love Nat King Cole. I love Michael Jordan. I just love him. We got a black guy works in management. Twenty-four million blacks living in poverty but it's their fault. Look, we got a black astronaut. I just love Oprah. How do you guys dance like that? After awhile that center starts to give. They keep making up the rules as you go along. They keep changing the maps. Then you realize you're never going to get to that center. It's all a house of cards. Everything resting on a slim edge. Looking back you can see it all. Wasn't nothing solid about it. Everything was an if and a when and a maybe. Of course ... but not really. Yes ... but not really. I don't want to live my life like that, Roosevelt.

The August Wilson Estate seeks to preserve and advance Mr. Wilson's universal legacy, including The American Century Cycle, by educating all people about his contribution to the American Theatre. Building on traditional interpretations, we encourage theatre artists to explore his plays through an ever-changing political, cultural, socioeconomic and artistic lens. We welcome the creation of deeper levels of meaning because we hold Mr. Wilson's words as an important affirmation of our humanity, which will guide us now and into the future.

Constanza Romero
Executor of the August Wilson Estate